P9-DMQ-006

TRUE SPIRITUALITY

FRANCIS A. SCHAEFFER

TRUE
SPIRITUALITY

TYNDALE HOUSE PUBLISHERS, WHEATON ILLINOIS

Visit Tyndale's exciting Web site at www.tyndale.com

Copyright © 1971, 2001 by Tyndale House Publishers, Inc. All rights reserved.

First printing 1971

Cover photograph copyright © 2001 by Stone. All rights reserved.

Designed by Dean H. Renninger

Scripture quotations are taken from the *Holy Bible,* King James Version.

Library of Congress Cataloging-in-Publication Data

Library of Congress Catalog Card Number 73—183269

ISBN 8423-7350-0, Cloth

8423-7351-9, Paper

Printed in the United States of America

06	05	04	03	02	01
36	35	34	33	32	

To My Very Good Friends

Edith
Priscilla and John
Susan and Ran
Elizabee
Margaret
Becky
Kirsty
Jandy
Fiona
Debby and Udo
Franky and Genie
Natasha
Jessica
Samantha

April 1971

CONTENTS

SECTION I: FREEDOM NOW FROM THE BONDS OF SIN

BASIC CONSIDERATIONS OF TRUE SPIRITUALITY

BIBLICAL UNITY AND TRUE SPIRITUALITY

MOMENT-BY-MOMENT PRACTICE OF TRUE SPIRITUALITY

SECTION II: FREEDOM NOW FROM THE RESULTS OF THE BONDS OF SIN

MAN'S SEPARATION FROM HIMSELF

MAN'S SEPARATION FROM HIS FELLOWMAN

FOREWORD

A biblical prophet, it has been said, is not one who sees into the future, as stargazers and crystal ball readers purport to do. Rather, he's one who sees things in the present that others are blind to. And a prophet is one who warns us of what will happen in the future if we don't mend our ways.

By that definition, Francis Schaeffer was the great prophet of the latter half of the twentieth century. He was God's most powerful voice to both church and culture.

Schaeffer saw things in the sixties and seventies that others didn't—or wouldn't—see. So he warned us that the great issue was truth—"true truth," or "flaming truth," as he used to cry out in his rasping, high-pitched voice.

Schaeffer saw that relativism and existentialism, advanced by European intellectuals, was infiltrating mainstream American thought. He argued eloquently, as well, that Christianity was a worldview, and he did so at a time when the Jesus movement was at its absolute peak; many people thought Jesus was the beginning and the end of the biblical account. Schaeffer talked about commitment and the authority of Scripture when all around us the institutions of authority were crumbling. He was, in short, *contra mundum,* or as one church declaration put it, "against the world for the world."

People came to hear him in droves, for he was a curiosity of sorts. He certainly made for a colorful figure, standing on the stage in his knickers and goatee, pleading with his audiences. He was an intellectual, but he preached like a revivalist. Thinking Christians heard his message and devoured his books; the drop-outs from the hippie culture of the sixties flocked to L'Abri, his retreat in the Swiss Alps. His provocative film series made the rounds of evangelical churches. But the ranks of evangelicals never really understood the full weight of what he preached.

Today, however, we all understand what Schaeffer and his disciples truly saw 40 years ago. The world today is awash in relativism. Seventy-two percent of the American people say there is no such thing as absolute truth. Even more shocking, 67 percent of evangelicals say there is no truth, while claiming to follow the One who says He is *the* truth! Despite the best efforts of some of us who have picked up on Schaeffer's teachings and themes, understanding of worldviews is still very limited in most evangelical circles. A quarter of born again Christians embrace New Age ideas like reincarnation.

Though I confess that I didn't understand it as well then as I do today, Schaeffer's message nonetheless struck home. His books and speeches helped launch me on an intellectual and spiritual quest. Since the mid-eighties, I have preached on worldview and the need to see Christianity as an integrated life system, as an explanation of all of reality. I have been so influenced by Schaeffer, in fact, that I dedicated my most recent book, written with my co-author Nancy Pearcey, to Francis Schaeffer. (Nancy, in fact, studied at L'Abri, and her experience there was instrumental in her conversion.)

Schaeffer was not only a great prophet and intellectual, but he was also a gracious and loving teacher. I first met him when I visited L'Abri in the late seventies, and then I spent many hours with him in the years that followed. I never failed to learn, never failed to be inspired. At one of the most stressful points in my ministry, I sought Schaeffer's counsel. His reply was, "Don't try to do everything. Every need is not a call." That particular advice liberated me.

It was advice Schaeffer lived. He avoided many distractions, carefully skirting political controversies that would not profit the Christian world. He concentrated on defending orthodoxy and truth, encouraging true spirituality, and advancing a Christian view of all of life. Schaeffer's message is enduring, his teaching as important to this generation as it was to the flower children and the evangelical church in the seventies.

The two books helpfully republished here are truly classics, each in its own way. *He Is There and He Is Not Silent* makes the fundamental Schaeffer case on the truth of biblical revelation and of the biblical understanding of life. It is masterful apologetics, providing a grand understanding of Christianity against the great philosophical trends and assaults of the modern age. *He Is There* is one of the most important of the many books he wrote of this genre. It will powerfully engage your mind (both the first time you read it and during subsequent readings, as I have discovered).

True Spirituality is entirely different. It seeks to ground the believer in true faith. It is a probing, penetrating search through the Scriptures for what it means to be truly Christian. Schaeffer himself said it should have been his first book, and he may have been right, for until you are grounded in the truth of God and are living it, you have nothing to defend in the marketplace of ideas. If *He Is There and He Is Not Silent* engages your mind, then *True Spirituality* will engage your heart.

This is a great combination of books, the two I would recommend of all the Schaeffer books to begin your study of this remarkable man's work. They give you both the spiritual and intellectual foundation to begin to think and behave Christianly in the world. The books are challenging and bracing reading—guaranteed to make you a Schaeffer devotee. That's good, because while we didn't listen well enough in the seventies, we can and must do so today.

The prophet speaks. There is still time.

Charles W. Colson
March 13, 2001
Washington, DC

INTRODUCTION

I wish to thank Tyndale House Publishers for the privilege of writing an introduction to this thirtieth anniversary edition of *True Spirituality*. Even though the first edition of this book was not published until 1971, its origin goes back much further in the life and ministry of Francis Schaeffer. Much of the material in the book is based on a series of lectures and sermons Schaeffer gave in the years 1953 and 1954, when he and his family were back in the United States on furlough from their ministry in Switzerland. While in the States, Schaeffer traveled extensively, and he spoke 346 times during a period of 515 days. Many of those talks were given on the subject of true spirituality.

Later, after the founding of L'Abri Fellowship in the Swiss village of Huémoz-sur-Ollon in 1955, Schaeffer would give lectures from time to time on the subject of the spiritual life, developing the talks first given back in the States. The lectures were eventually tape-recorded and became one of the foundational tape series of L'Abri's library that people would listen to when they were students in Huémoz.

It was through one of those students that I was converted in the fall of 1966, while I was an undergraduate at Manchester University in the north of England. I became a believer primarily through the life and ministry of Michael Tymchak, a Canadian who had studied at the Swiss L'Abri and who was deeply influenced by the teaching of Francis Schaeffer. Mike invited Schaeffer to come and speak at Manchester, and so I first heard Schaeffer lecture in person a few months before my own conversion. Mike also used to have a discussion meeting at his apartment during which he would either give a Bible study or play a taped lecture by Schaeffer. That was the context in which I became a believer, with the Lord using Schaeffer's teaching ministry in a significant way in my own life. A few months after my conversion, I graduated from Manchester, and the next day I hitchhiked to Huémoz to study and to help in the branch of L'Abri there.

While working as Edith Schaeffer's cook and gardener in the fall of 1967, I listened to the lectures that were to become *True Spirituality,* and as for many others who studied at L'Abri, those lectures became cornerstones of my own understanding of the Christian life. Eventually, so many believers found the lectures so helpful, and so many expressed deep thankfulness to the Lord for their content, that Schaeffer was encouraged to put them into book form.

However, the origin of the studies that eventually found their way into *True Spirituality* goes back further than that speaking tour in the United States in 1953–1954. In the winter months of late 1950 and early 1951, Schaeffer went through a profound spiritual crisis that was, in God's providence, to shape his whole future life and ministry. As he wrote in the preface to the first edition of *True Spirituality,* "I realized that in honesty I had to go back and rethink my whole position. I had to go all the way back to my agnosticism." Edith Schaeffer gives a much more detailed account of this difficult period in their lives in her book *The Tapestry* (354-356), but I heard Francis talk about his crisis on many occasions. To understand the seriousness and urgency of the problems he faced, we need to see whereabouts in the history of his life and ministry the difficulties that were so troubling to him came to a head.

Schaeffer was converted in 1930, at the age of seventeen. Not long after becoming a believer he felt called to the ministry of the Word and enrolled in a pre-ministerial degree program at Hampden-Sydney College in Virginia. While a student there he met Edith, and they were married shortly after his graduation. He then enrolled at Westminster Seminary in Philadelphia in 1935 to begin his theological training, though he completed his studies at Faith Seminary in Wilmington, Delaware.

After serving three different churches in the United States, two in Pennsylvania and one in Missouri, Francis and Edith were called to serve in Switzerland from 1948 onward. These intervening years had seen involvement in several different ministries. They had started a ministry to children, Children for Christ, while they were in their third pastoral position in St. Louis, Missouri. This eventually became international, and the Bible studies they wrote for children were translated into many languages. They personally helped to train leaders of evangelistic children's Bible studies in several different countries.

In addition to the children's ministry and his pastoral work, Schaeffer was also involved in the International Council of Christian Churches, a separatist body formed to stand for biblical orthodoxy over against the World Council of Churches. Participation in the ICCC led Schaeffer into speaking and writing against the influence of liberal theology in the wider church and in particular against neoorthodoxy. Francis and Edith had been sent to Europe by their denominational mission board with the call "to strengthen the things that remain." He had traveled in Europe for several months in 1947, seeking to understand and evaluate the state of the European church in the years after World War II, and their being "sent" arose from the impact of the reports he had written about what he had discovered.

Once settled in Europe, Francis and Edith devoted themselves to a variety of ministries: evangelism, training others to lead evangelistic studies for children, speaking and writing against theological liberalism, and Bible teaching and hospitality. It was after approximately three years of ministry in Switzerland that Schaeffer felt he had to "go back to the beginning and think his faith through all over again."

What brought on his spiritual crisis? Going back many years to his time in college, and later in seminary, Francis and Edith were bothered by the lack of love shown between Christians, especially where there was any disagreement. The denomination of which they were a part had been formed by a split from the Northern Presbyterian Church, which occurred in response to an influx of liberalism and the defrocking of J. Gresham Machen when he started an independent mission board to ensure that the missionaries sent overseas were Bible-believing

Christians. This new church experienced a subsequent division into two denominations within a year of the first split. Schaeffer was a student during these divisions and had joined the part that started Faith Seminary in Wilmington, Delaware. At that time Francis and Edith wrestled with this question: "How could people stand for God's holiness and the purity of doctrine in the church, and in one's personal life, and yet not have it turn out to be harsh and ugly?" (*The Tapestry* 189).

By 1951 Schaeffer felt he had seen so much that was harsh and ugly within "the separated movement" that he was not sure he could in honesty be a Christian any longer. He saw so much that was negative, so much that defined Christian orthodoxy primarily in terms of what it was "against." He saw so much infighting within the circles of which he was a part, in his own denomination and across large segments of the evangelical community. He saw men struggling for power and using unscrupulous methods to gain or to maintain control and positions of influence. He wondered what they were "for," and what affirmations there were to set alongside the negations. Where was the passion for evangelism that fills the pages of the New Testament? Where was the devotional literature expressing love for the Lord? Where were the hymns that would demonstrate that the imagination and the heart were being touched by God's truth along with the mind? Where was love for fellow believers and for one's unbelieving neighbors that would show to the world that the Father sent the Son for our salvation? Where was the spiritual reality that fills the pages of the book of Acts and of the New Testament Epistles?

He was not only dissatisfied with the circles of which they were a part. He said "Edith, I feel really torn to pieces by the lack of reality, the lack of seeing the results the Bible talks about, which should be seen in the Lord's people. I'm not talking only about people I'm working with in 'The Movement,' but I'm not satisfied with myself. It seems that the only honest thing to do is to rethink, reexamine the whole matter of Christianity. Is it true? I need to go back to my agnosticism and start at the beginning" (*The Tapestry* 355-357). Edith writes about her prayers for Francis during these months of questioning as he would take extended walks in the mountains around their village, or on rainy days pace up and down in the attic of the barn next to their home.

He went through a period lasting several months, during which he reread the Bible and thought through the most basic questions about our human situation all over again. Once again, just as when he first was converted, he found his answers in the unfolding of God's revelation of himself in what he would later call "the flow of biblical history" (see, e.g., chapter 1 of *Genesis in Space and Time* [Downers Grove: InterVarsity Press, 1972]). By the end of this time, "the sun came out and the song came. . . . Interestingly enough, although I had written no poetry for many years, in that time of joy and song I found poetry beginning to flow again—poetry of certainty, an affirmation of life, thanksgiving, and praise. Admittedly, as poetry it is very poor, but it expressed a song in my heart that was wonderful to me" (Preface to *True Spirituality*). He was ready to write and to pray:

> *Come Christian Triune God who lives,*
> *Shake the world again!*

What did he discover as the Lord brought him out of this crisis?

1. He found a solid foundation for his own faith and life. He became convinced again that the Bible answers the most basic questions that all human persons ask. This gave him a delight in the biblical message as the source of the only true explanation of our existence.

2. He developed a confidence in Scripture as the sure and inerrant Word of God. This confidence in the Scripture would, in God's providence, be of enormous help to him in the work the Lord was preparing for him. As God knew, in the years to come, he would be inundated with the questions of unbelievers. From then on he would take the questions and doubts that unbelievers raise against the Bible very seriously, and he would answer them with gentleness and compassion and deep

understanding. Whatever criticisms they might make of the church if they had seen ugliness and a lack of love, he would listen to with a sympathetic ear, and without being defensive, for he had seen that ugliness himself.

3. In the same way, he was being prepared to deal with the great barrage of questions, doubts, and hurts that would come at him from Christians who were struggling with their faith, for in the years to come many of these would come to his home at L'Abri. No questions were off-limits, and doubts and hurts were taken seriously, for he knew only too well himself that a Christian could be on the verge of giving up their faith.

4. Prayer became much more real to him and far more important in his own life. He would often say, "How many churches and ministries would not even notice and would carry on in exactly the same manner as usual, even though every reference to dependence on the Holy Spirit and to prayer were suddenly to disappear from the pages of the New Testament!"

5. He also "discovered" that the central, unfolding theme of God's revelation is the love shown by God to us, and the trusting and dependent love that we are called to show him in return.

He wrote, after this crisis experience, an article in two parts for the *Sunday School Times:* "The Secret of Power and the Enjoyment of the Lord" (June 16 and July 8, 1951). Schaeffer would often say in later years that this brief article was one of the most important things he ever wrote. Its central themes are developed at much greater length in the lectures that lie behind *True Spirituality.*

His starting point is the lack of power that is so common in the lives of Bible-believing Christians, and also the lack of enjoyment of a relationship with the Lord. He saw these weaknesses not only in individuals, but also in organizations, and he saw them in himself—"my own reality was less than it had been in the early days after I had become a Christian" (Preface to *True Spirituality*).

What did he mean by "power"? He meant a lack of fruitfulness: people's own lives being transformed, and other people's lives being touched, saved, and transformed. Yet the apostle Paul teaches us that the gospel is the "power of God unto salvation" (Romans 1:16). What did he mean by "enjoyment"? He saw that there were many rules for Christians to live by, but there was a lack of joy in the lives of believers. Yet the apostle Paul declares that the "kingdom of God is not a matter of eating and drinking, but of righteousness, peace and joy in the Holy Spirit" (Romans 14:17, NIV).

Schaeffer begins his reflections on these issues, both in the article and in *True Spirituality*, at a point where every Christian will agree with him. We are born again through faith in Christ and then we are called to purity of life. But then a question arises. How do we understand purity? Is purity simply giving up certain amusements and habits, a list of do's and don'ts that are primarily negative (such as rules about appropriate books, music, movies; rules about drinking, smoking, dancing, card-playing, gambling, and various obviously worldly pursuits)? Purity, he argues, while it might include some of these things, is actually far deeper than such minutiae of the law that the Pharisees majored on in Jesus' day, and that Christians so easily major on today.

These external rules are relatively easy to keep, and focusing on them has the effect of hiding us from the true requirements of God's law. These outward rules replace God's law with "the screen of a trite list," and then I easily become proud and think that I am doing very well as a Christian. All these things are outward, and while the law of God does speak about outward matters, the ones it emphasizes are adultery, theft, and false testimony, and these are far weightier than the rules that Christians can preoccupy themselves with observing.

But there is more to purity than even these "weightier" outward matters, for God's law focuses on the inward matters, on the heart and its attitudes. The tenth commandment is about covetousness and is entirely inward, and it applies to all the other commandments. Coveting is the reverse side of the law of love. Do I love God with heart and soul and mind and strength, or do I covet against God; that is, do I desire "God's prerogatives for myself?" Do I worship and serve myself, and pursue my own desires for comfort, pleasure and security, or do I worship and serve the Lord himself? Do I love my neighbor as myself, or do I covet against my neighbor? Do I desire what he has and envy him for his gifts, possessions, or leadership? Would I secretly rejoice if he lost his position of leadership, or be wretched inwardly if he gained recognition that I do not receive? When there is such "coveting" there is no purity.

Schaeffer saw so much that was truly "worldly" in the leadership battles of the movement of which he was a part, and this was one of the problems of lack of reality that had distressed him so deeply and had contributed to his crisis. (Ironically, his giving this "new teaching" on spirituality during his furlough in the States was seen as a bid for leadership by some within "the movement"!)

Purity, however, goes even deeper than a lack of this internal coveting. Purity is about the positive reverse of coveting; it is about love, loving God with my whole being and loving my neighbor as myself. The same is true with purity of the church. Purity of the church is not simply about disciplining those who teach false doctrine, or who are morally disobedient, or separating oneself from them when discipline is no longer possible. The end of the purity of the visible church must not be purity itself, but rather love for the Lord and a desire to please Him.

Church discipline by itself is not a sign of vitality, life, and power, for separation must not be just separation from unbelief and immorality, but separation to God. Without a deep love for God there is only division—not a biblical purity and true separation—and then whatever orthodoxy of doctrine we may think we have, all we truly have is something that is of the "flesh," of the sinful nature, something worldly.

At the heart of "The Secret of Power and the Enjoyment of the Lord" is a discourse on love, and this theme is also developed as a recurring refrain throughout *True Spirituality*. God calls us to love, and not only love for those who are in our little portion of God's church, or even for all our fellow Christians, but love for all people, unbelievers as well as believers. Schaeffer saw that there was, at that time, a tendency to minimize the challenge of the parable of the Good Samaritan, and to focus the love of Christians on those who are fighting alongside us in the Lord's battles.

We face the same problem today, for the more secularized and "post-Christian" our society becomes, the greater temptation there is to love only our fellow believers who are fighting by our side in the "culture wars." We retreat from the command to love all people as we consider those outside the church as too worldly, as too dangerous to our spiritual well-being. Rather than loving them, we feel constrained to keep ourselves separate from them, to strive for a purity of being uncontaminated by having no contact with the "sinners" out there. But, as Schaeffer points out, this is not the kind of purity that God's Word has in mind for us. The Lord calls us to love all people, including those who are encmies of the gospel and those who blaspheme. This may not be comfortable, and it may not be easy, but this is the gospel of Christ, for He loved His enemies so much that He died to save us.

Love, Schaeffer says, cannot be a banner that we carry around, or a slogan that we repeat like a mantra. Love must be evident in practice. All truly great Christians, he writes, have a gentleness and tenderness about them, a gentleness and tenderness that is manifest in the delight they take in spending time with little children and the energy they gladly expend on "little people." Such love demonstrates that a believer truly has met with the Lord. For the Lord carries little children close to his heart. The Lord does not break "the bruised reed" or quench "the smoldering wick." The Lord has time for every one of his people - no matter how insignificant they may seem to the Christian leader who has his own big agenda in mind.

This emphasis on gentleness and tenderness was one that was deeply engraved on Schaeffer's mind and heart. To those of us who worked with him day by day, this is what we saw in his own life. His eyes would go soft at the sight of a little child. He would show tender compassion to people struggling with their doubts and questions. He would gladly sit and talk for hours to someone the world (or the church) might consider insignificant. He was just as happy talking with the maid or the janitor in a hotel as he was meeting famous church, business, or political leaders.

Love, he wrote, must be evident in practice; love must be shown in acts of kindness in the small and large things of each day, in fair dealing with everyone—including those who make themselves our personal enemies or the enemies of the gospel. We can become so involved in the battle for the truth, or the battle for "family values," that we begin to act as if any means are permissible to advance our cause. We indulge in character assassination, misrepresentation, politicizing, lobbying, bending the rules, and being so scrupulously law-abiding to our "rules of order" that we ensure that we get our way. We have our own sanitized versions of political "smoke-filled rooms" to win the votes, and we justify all such practices by comforting ourselves with the thought that we are fighting the Lord's cause for him. If this is what we are doing, then we are not doing the Lord's work in the Lord's way. Rather, love is gone, and spiritual power is gone; all that is left is sinful, worldly, self-centered human effort. There is no power of God when we behave in such ways, even if we are convinced our cause is right and godly. All such practice is "man-centered." Then, dead orthodoxy is just a breath away from us, a form of godliness without its power.

Schaeffer was not "going soft" on sin or unbelief when he wrote about such problems. He insisted that we must be prepared to discipline false teaching, that "purity" requires a readiness to talk about failures to be faithful to God's Word and to his commandments. But he was contending for the recognition that a passion for purity must work itself out in holiness in our own lives, genuine holiness that will be seen in a growing love for God and for all around us.

If there is biblical purity, then there will be not only contending for the faith against false teaching and unbelief, but also an outpouring of devotional literature, hymns, and devotional sermons. If there is true purity, then there will also be a growing reality of prayer in public and in private. Any commitment to purity must arise out of a deepening love for Christ, not a desire for honor, leadership, or money, and especially not a desire for power. It was this hunger for power among Christian leaders that had so soured his own confidence in the gospel that he had to go back to the beginning and think everything through again.

If we love Christ more than ourselves, then we must be ready to fight against the longing to be proved right, against the hunger for honor, for praise, for leadership, for money, for power—and we must fight this battle daily in the power of the Spirit. If we love Christ, then we must be prepared to die daily, to put all such thoughts (for power, money, leadership, etc.) to death for the sake of love for him. This emphasis on the need to "die daily" is one of the major themes of *True Spirituality*, and it is still a message that is rarely taught in our churches. We love to think well of ourselves and to find reason to congratulate ourselves on our devoted service to the Lord, but Schaeffer's emphasis on being ruthlessly honest about the motivations of our hearts does not leave room for such self-congratulation.

Instead, such an emphasis drives us to recognize our ongoing need for the mercy of Christ and for his empowerment in our lives. This is what *True Spirituality* is primarily about, the importance of living by faith in the work of Christ on a daily basis. We can only be justified by faith in Christ, and all true Christians acknowledge this gladly, for we recognize that we can never offer to God sufficient righteousness to make ourselves acceptable to him. But, says Schaeffer (and this is the testimony of the whole of Scripture!), we are also to be sanctified by faith. Living as a Christian is not getting through a door by believing in Jesus and then proceeding by our own efforts as if we could readily sanctify ourselves. No! Sanctification, Christian growth, is a work of God's Spirit, a work to be appropriated by faith – just as much as our initial salvation is a work of God that is received by faith.

What will this mean? Schaeffer repeatedly appeals to the example of Mary to help us to see what God intends for us. When the angel Gabriel came to Mary to announce to her that she would conceive a child, she did not respond: "Great! I will do this task myself!" Rather, she replied in humility: "I am the Lord's servant. May it be to me as you have said" (Luke 1:38)

Schaeffer coins the phrase "active passivity" to try to express what is happening here. Mary yields herself to God for him to do his work in her body, and in this way she is passive; but this is not the passivity of resignation, of inactivity, for there is the exercise of her faith. Mary believes God's promise and acts upon it by gladly yielding herself to the Lord that she might be his servant. This is to be our calling every day. We are to trust that God will do his work in us by the agency of his Holy Spirit, and we are to yield ourselves to him that he might bear the fruit of righteousness, love, joy, patience, and peace in our lives.

Schaeffer loves this example of Mary, for it ties in with a biblical image that he also delights to use. Christ is the Bridegroom and we are his bride. We cannot bear fruit by ourselves, just as Mary could not bear the Christ child by herself; rather, we only bear fruit as we love him and give ourselves to him.

One of Schaeffer's favorite passages of Scripture that expresses this truth was the Servant Song of Isaiah, found in chapter 50. In Isaiah's messianic poem the servant, Christ, says this,

> The sovereign Lord has given me an instructed tongue,
> to know the word that sustains the weary.
> He wakens me morning by morning,
> wakens my ear to listen like one being taught. (Isaiah 50:4, NIV)

Later in the chapter, those who follow the servant are admonished to imitate his example of speaking the words of the Lord, rather than their own words, his example of trusting in God, rather than relying on themselves.

> Who among you fears the Lord and obeys the word of his
> servant?
> Let him who walks in the dark, who has no light,
> trust in the name of the Lord and rely on his God.

But now, all you who light fires and provide yourselves with
flaming torches,
go, walk in the light of your fires and of the torches you
have set ablaze.
This is what you shall receive from my hand: You will lie
down in torment. (Isaiah 50:10-11, NIV)

Schaeffer was passionate about these words. He knew that only God can establish what we do, only God can teach us what to say, only God can lead us where we should go, and only God is sufficient for the challenges we face. He wanted to do the Lord's work in the Lord's way. He wanted to make a distinction between people, or rather, he observed that there is a distinction between professing Christians. On the one hand are people who think they are building God's kingdom for him (and therefore end up building their own kingdoms). On the other hand are people who pray that God will build his kingdom and will be pleased to use them as he does. This second way, Schaeffer believed with every fiber of his being, is the message of the God who has created us, the God against whom we have rebelled, the God who has come to deliver us from judgment and from dependence on ourselves. Words almost exactly like these about "building God's kingdom" are written into the consensus that governs the mentality of those who work at the various branches of L'Abri. It is this "active passivity" of choosing to trust in God, of asking him to do the work of the church and of the kingdom, and of yielding ourselves to him for him to do his work in and through us, that is a constantly recurring theme in *True Spirituality*.

One of the great difficulties we face is the pressure of the secular society in which we live. The very air we breathe teaches us that we are living in a universe in which God is inactive. Yet the Scripture teaches us that we live in a universe in which God is constantly at work. Schaeffer asks us whether we will sit in the chair of the "materialist," who does not believe in the intervention of God, or in the chair of the person who knows that God is ceaselessly at work in our lives and in this world? He reminds us that our lives and our faith are on display before the angels. They are watching eagerly to see whether we will trust God "moment by moment," or whether we will live the Christian life as if we were dependent merely on our own efforts.

This example of the "universe and two chairs" leads me to comment on one of the unique aspects of the teaching of Francis Schaeffer. It is this constant bringing together of the biblical message and the challenge of the thought forms of the culture in which we live. In every sermon, in every Bible study, in every lecture (no matter what the subject), in every discussion, he would help us to see both what the Bible teaches, and how the biblical message is threatened or undermined by the ideas and practices of the culture in which we live. So, all the way through *True Spirituality,* the reader will find this regular interaction with the ideas of the world around. Some of Schaeffer's comments will ring a bell for those who are familiar with "New Age" thinking, though he does not use that term, as such thinking was not as wildly popular then as it is now, thirty years on. However, he is responding already to these ideas and beliefs that were beginning to be heard back in the late sixties and early seventies.

In this constant interaction with the culture, Schaeffer is seeking to help Christians be obedient to Paul's injunction in Romans 12:1-2: "Do not conform any longer to the pattern of this world, but be transformed by the renewing of your mind" (NIV). As we do this, we may more readily present ourselves to the Lord as living sacrifices for him to do his work in and through us.

When there is a growing reality of offering ourselves to God in this way, then, says Schaeffer, there will be "substantial healing" in our lives now. He means by this phrase that there will indeed be genuine changes in our lives because God will be at work in us when we live by faith in the completed work that Christ has done for us. There will be "substantial healing" because there is more than just our longing to change and our efforts to change. God himself is changing us. He will begin to bring healing to our psychological problems. He will begin to wipe away our tears. He will begin to heal our relationships with others within the church. He will begin to make us a blessing, a "song of life," to the society around us.

This substantial healing will be a demonstration of the existence of God to believers and to unbelievers. As he often used to say, non-Christians ought to be able to see "supernaturally restored relationships" when they observe the lives of Christians. In chapter 12 of this book he writes: "How beautiful Christianity is – first because of the sparkling quality of its intellectual answers, but secondly because of the beautiful quality of its human and personal answers" (144). In our postmodern culture, people doubt the existence of sparkling intellectual answers until they see the beautiful quality of the human and personal answers in our lives. Unless they see "supernaturally restored relationships," unless they see a "song of life" they are unlikely to pay attention to any proclamation of the gospel.

Francis Schaeffer sought to practice this as well as to teach it. In L'Abri Fellowship he and Edith desired and prayed that God would build a work that would indeed demonstrate his existence. They longed for an intellectual demonstration as people's questions were answered from God's Word. They longed for a living demonstration in the community life of God doing his work of sanctifying and restoring his people. They longed for a demonstration of God answering prayers–and that by means of this tapestry of truth, life, and prayer, God would be pleased to draw men and women to himself through faith in Christ. Francis knew that these things would never be perfect in this life because of the spiritual poverty of all of us as God's people, but he trusted that God would delight to do His work of "substantial healing" anyway. "This work [of seeking to lead people to faith in Christ, and of trying to help them lead holy lives] is impossible for us," he would often say. "But God is at work doing what we can never do." It was Francis Schaeffer's earnest conviction that we need to depend on the work that God does in our lives. This is the heart of *True Spirituality*. It is my prayer that the Lord will be pleased to use this new edition of this book to teach this truth to a new generation of believers.

Jerram Barrs
March 2001

PREFACE

This book is being published after a number of others, but in a certain sense it should have been my first. Without the material in this book there would be no L'Abri. In 1951 and 1952 I faced a spiritual crisis in my own life. I had become a Christian from agnosticism many years before. After that I had become a pastor for ten years in the United States, and then for several years my wife Edith and I had been working in Europe. During this time I felt a strong burden to stand for the historical Christian position and for the purity of the visible Church. Gradually, however, a problem came to me—the problem of reality. This had two parts: first, it seemed to me that among many of those who held the orthodox position one saw little reality in the things that the Bible so clearly said should be the result of Christianity. Second, it gradually grew on me that my own reality was less than it had been in the early days after I had become a Christian. I realized that in honesty I had to go back and rethink my whole position.

We were living in Champèry at that time, and I told Edith that for the sake of honesty, I had to go all the way back to my agnosticism and think through the whole matter. I'm sure that this was a difficult time for her and I'm sure that she prayed much for me in those days. I walked in the mountains when it was clear, and when it was rainy I walked backward and forward in the hayloft of the old chalet in which we lived. I walked, prayed, and thought through what the Scriptures taught, reviewing my own reasons for being a Christian.

As I rethought my reasons for being a Christian, I saw again that there were totally sufficient reasons to know that the infinite-personal God does exist and that Christianity is true. In going further, I saw something else which made a profound difference in my life. I searched through what the Bible said concerning reality as a Christian. Gradually I saw that the problem was that with all the teaching I had received after I was a Christian, I had heard little about what the Bible says about the meaning of the finished work of Christ for our present lives. Gradually the sun came out and the song came. Interestingly enough, although I had written no poetry for many years, in that time of joy and song I found poetry beginning to flow again—poetry of certainty, an affirmation of life, thanksgiving, and praise. Admittedly, as poetry it is very poor, but it expressed a song in my heart that was wonderful to me.

This was and is the real basis of L'Abri. Teaching the historic Christian answers and giving honest answers to honest questions are crucial, but it was out of these struggles that the reality came, without which an incisive work like L'Abri would not have been possible. I, and we, can only be thankful.

These principles, which I worked out in Champèry, were first delivered as talks at a Bible camp in an old barn in Dakota. This was in July of 1953. They were worked out on scraps of paper in the pastor's basement. The Lord gave something very special from these messages, and I'm still meeting those who as young people had their thinking and their lives changed there. After L'Abri began in 1955, I preached these same messages in Huémoz in the late winter and early spring of 1964. This was their final form and the form in which they are recorded on the L'Abri tapes. The Lord has used the tapes in a way that has moved us deeply, not only with those with spiritual problems, but also for many who had psychological needs as well. We pray that this written form of these studies will be as useful as the tapes have been in many parts of the world.

Huémoz, Switzerland
May 1971

FREEDOM NOW FROM THE BONDS OF SIN

CHAPTER 1

THE LAW AND
THE LAW OF LOVE

The question before us is what the Christian life, true spirituality, really is, and how it may be lived in a twentieth-century setting.

The first point that we must make is that it is impossible even to begin living the Christian life, or to know anything of true spirituality, before one is a Christian. And the only way to become a Christian is neither by trying to live some sort of a Christian life nor by hoping for some sort of religious experience, but rather by accepting Christ as Savior. No matter how complicated, educated, or sophisticated we may be, or how simple we may be, we must all come the same way, insofar as becoming a Christian is concerned. As the kings of the earth and the mighty of the earth are born in exactly the same way, physically, as the simplest man, so the most intellectual person must become a Christian in exactly the same way as the simplest person. This is true for all men everywhere, through all space and all time. There are no exceptions. Jesus said a totally exclusive word: "No man cometh unto the Father, but by me" (John 14:6).

The reason for this is that all men are separated from God because of their true moral guilt. God exists, God has a character, God is a holy God; and when men sin (and we all must acknowledge we have sinned not only by mistake but by intention), they have true moral guilt before the God who exists. That guilt is not just the modern concept of guilt-feelings, a psychological guilty feeling in man. It is a true moral guilt before the infinite-personal, holy God. Only the finished, substitutionary work of Christ upon the cross as the Lamb of God—in history, space, and time—is enough to remove this. Our true guilt, that brazen heaven which stands between us and God, can be removed only upon the basis of the finished work of Christ *plus nothing* on our part. The Bible's whole emphasis is that there must be no humanistic note added at any point in the accepting of the gospel. It is the infinite value of the finished work of Christ, the second person of the Trinity, upon the cross *plus nothing* that is the sole basis for the removal of our guilt. When we thus come, believing God, the Bible says we are declared justified by God, the guilt is gone, and we are returned to fellowship with God—the very thing for which we were created in the first place.

Just as the only *basis* for the removal of our guilt is the finished work of Christ upon the cross in history, plus nothing, so the only *instrument* for accepting that finished work of Christ upon the cross is faith. This is not faith in the twentieth-century or Kierkegaardian concept of faith as a jump in the dark—not a solution on the basis of faith in faith. It is believing the specific promises of God; no longer turning our backs on them, no longer calling God a liar, but raising the empty hands of faith and accepting that finished work of Christ as it was fulfilled in history upon the cross. The Bible says that at that moment we pass from death to life, from the kingdom of darkness to the kingdom of God's dear Son. We become, individually, children of God. We are children of God from that time on. I repeat, there is no way to begin the Christian life except through the door of spiritual birth, any more than there is any other way to begin physical life except through the door of physical birth.

Yet, having said this about the beginning of the Christian life, we must also realize that while the new birth is necessary as the beginning, it is only the beginning. We must not think that because we have accepted Christ as Savior and are therefore Christians, this is all there is in the Christian life. In one way physical birth is the most important part in our physical life, because we are not alive in the external world until we have been born. In another way, however, it is the least important of all the aspects of our life, because it is only the beginning and then it is past. After we are born, the important thing is the living of our life in all its relationships, possibilities, and capabilities. It is exactly the same with the new birth. In one way, the new birth is the most important thing in our spiritual life, because we are not Christians until we have come this way. In another way, however, *after* one has become a Christian, it must be minimized, in that we should not always have our mind only on our new birth. The important thing after being born spiritually is to live. There is a new birth, and *then* there is the Christian life to be lived. This is the area of sanctification, from the time of the new birth through this present life, until Jesus comes or until we die.

Often, after a person is born again and asks, "What shall I do next?" he is given a list of things, usually of a limited nature and primarily negative. Often he is given the idea that if he does not do this series of things (whatever this series of things happens to be in the particular country and location and at the time he happens to live), he will be spiritual. This is not so. The true Christian life, *true spirituality*, is not merely a negative not-doing of any small list of things. Even if the list began as a very excellent list of things to beware of in that particular historic setting, we still must emphasize that the Christian life, or true spirituality, is more than refraining from a certain list of external taboos in a mechanical way.

Because this is true, there almost always comes into being another group of Christians that rises up and begins to work against such a list of taboos; thus, there is a tendency toward a struggle in Christian circles between those who set up a certain list of taboos and those who, feeling there is something wrong with this, say, "Away with all taboos, away with all lists." Both of these groups can be right and both can be wrong, depending on how they approach the matter.

I was impressed by this on one Saturday night at L'Abri, when we were having one of our discussion times. On that particular night everybody present was a Christian, many of them from groups in countries where "lists" had been very much accentuated. They began to talk against the use of taboos, and at first as I listened to them I rather agreed with them, in the direction they were going. But as I listened further to this conversation, and as they spoke against the taboos in their own countries, it became quite clear to me that what they really wanted was merely to be able to do the things that the taboos were against. What they really wanted was a more lax Christian life. But we must see that in giving up such lists, in feeling the limitation of the "list" mentality, we must not do this merely in order to be able to live a looser life; it must be for something deeper. So I think both sides of this discussion can be right and both sides can be wrong. We do not come to true spirituality or the true Christian life merely by keeping a list, but neither do we come to it merely by rejecting the list and then shrugging our shoulders and living a looser life.

If we are considering outward things in relation to true spirituality, we are face-to-face not with some small list, but with the whole Ten Commandments and all of God's other commands. In other words, if I see the list as a screen, and I say this small list is trite, dead, and cheap, and I take hold of the screen and lift it away, then I am not face-to-face with a looser thing; I am face-to-face with the whole Ten Commandments and all that is included in them. I am also face-to-face with what we might call the Law of Love, the fact that I am to love God and I am to love my fellowman.

In the book of Romans, in the fourteenth chapter, verse fifteen, we read:

"But if thy brother be grieved with thy meat, now walkest thou not charitably. Destroy not him with thy meat, for whom Christ died." This is the law of God. In a very real sense there is no liberty here. It is an absolute declaration that we are to do this. It is perfectly true that we cannot be saved by doing this, we cannot do this in our own strength, and none of us do this perfectly in this life. Nevertheless, it is an imperative. It is the absolute command of God. The same thing is true in 1 Corinthians 8:12-13: "But when ye sin so against the brethren, and wound their weak conscience, ye sin against Christ. Wherefore, if meat make my brother to offend, I will eat no flesh while the world standeth, lest I make my brother to offend." Therefore, when I take hold of the screen of a trite list and say, "This is too superficial," and I push it aside, I must see what I am doing. I am not now confronted with a libertine concept, but I am confronted with the whole Ten Commandments and with the Law of Love. So even if we are dealing only with *outward* commands, we have not moved into a looser life; we have moved into something much more profound and heart-searching. As a matter of fact, when we are done with our honest wrestling before God, very often we will find that we will be observing at least some of the taboos on these lists. But having gone deeper, we find that we will be observing them for a completely different reason. Curiously enough we often come around in a circle through our liberty, through the study of the deeper teaching, and find we do want to keep these things. But now *not* for the same reason—that of social pressure. It is no longer merely a matter of holding to an accepted list in order that Christians will think well of us.

However, eventually the Christian life and true spirituality are not to be seen as outward at all, but *inward*. The climax of the Ten Commandments is the tenth commandment in Exodus 20:17: "Thou shalt not covet thy neighbor's house, thou shalt not covet thy neighbor's wife, nor his manservant, nor his maidservant, nor his ox, nor his ass, nor any thing that is thy neighbor's." The commandment not to covet is an entirely inward thing. Coveting is never an outward thing, from the very nature of the case. It is an intriguing factor that this is the last command that God gives us in the Ten Commandments and thus the hub of the whole matter. The end of the whole thing is that we arrive at an inward situation and not merely an outward one. Actually, we break this last commandment, not to covet, before we break any of the others. Any time that we break one of the other commandments of God, it means that we have already broken this commandment in coveting. It also means that any time we break one of the others, we break this last commandment as well. So no matter which of the other Ten

Commandments you break, you break two: the commandment itself, and this commandment not to covet. This is the hub of the wheel.

In Romans 7:7-9, Paul states very clearly that this was the commandment which gave him a sense of being sinful:

> *What shall we say then? Is the law sin? God forbid. Nay, I had not known sin, but by the law: for I had not known lust except the law had said, Thou shalt not covet. But sin, taking occasion by the commandment, wrought in me all manner of concupiscence. For without the law sin was dead. For I was alive without the law once: but when the commandment came, sin revived, and I died.*

Now he did not mean he was perfect before; this is clear from what Paul has said. What he is saying here is, "I did not know I was a sinner; I thought I would come out all right, because I was keeping these outward things and was getting along all right in comparison with other people." He would have been measuring himself against the externalized form of the commandments that the Jews had in their tradition. But when he opened the Ten Commandments and read that the last commandment was not to covet, he saw he was a sinner. When did this take place? He does not tell us, but personally I feel that God was working inwardly in him and making him feel this lack even before the experience on the Damascus road—that already he had seen he was a sinner and had been troubled in the light of the tenth commandment—and then Christ spoke to him.

Coveting is the negative side of the positive commands, "Thou shalt love the Lord thy God with all thy heart, and with all thy soul, and with all thy mind. . . . [And] thou shalt love thy neighbour as thyself" (Matthew 22:37, 39).

Love is internal, not external. There can be external manifestations, but love itself will always be an internal factor. Coveting is always internal; the external manifestation is a result. We must see that to love God with all the heart, mind, and soul is not to covet against God; and to love man, to love our neighbor as ourselves, is not to covet against man. When I do not love the Lord as I should, I am coveting against the Lord. And when I do not love my neighbor as I should, I am coveting against him.

"Thou shalt not covet" is the internal commandment that shows the man who thinks himself to be moral that he really needs a Savior. The average such "moral" man, who has lived comparing himself to other men and comparing himself to a rather easy list of rules (even if they cause him some pain and difficulty), can feel, like Paul, that he is getting along all right. But suddenly, when he is confronted with the inward command not to covet, he is brought to his knees. It is exactly the same with us as Christians. This is a very central concept if we are to have any understanding or any real practice of the true Christian life or true spirituality. I can take lists that men make and I can seem to keep them, but to do that, my heart does not have to be bowed. But when I come to the inward aspect of the Ten Commandments, when I come to the inward aspect of the Law of Love, if I am listening even in a poor fashion to the direction of the Holy Spirit, I can no longer feel proud. I am brought to my knees. In this life I can never say, "I have arrived; it is finished; look at me—I am holy." When we talk of the Christian life or true spirituality, when we talk about freedom from the bonds of sin, we must be wrestling with the inward problems of not coveting against God and men, of loving God and men, and not merely some set of externals.

This immediately raises a question. Does this mean that *any* desire is coveting and therefore sinful? The Bible makes plain that this is not so—all desire is not sin. So then the question arises, when does proper desire become coveting? I think we can put the answer down simply: desire becomes sin when it fails to include love of God or men. Further, I think there are two practical tests as to when we are coveting against God or men; first, I am to love God enough to be contented; second, I am to love men enough not to envy.

Let us pursue these two tests. First, in regard to God: I am to love God enough to be contented, because otherwise even our natural and proper desires bring us into revolt against God. God has made us with proper desires, but if there is not a proper contentment on my part, to this extent I am in revolt against God, and of course revolt is the whole central problem of sin. When I lack proper contentment, either I have forgotten that God is God, or I have ceased to be submissive to him. We are now speaking about a practical test to judge if we are coveting against God. A quiet disposition and a heart giving thanks at any given moment is the real test of the extent to which we love God at that moment. I would like to give some strong words to you from the Bible to remind us that this is God's own standard for Christians: "But fornication, and all uncleanness, or covetousness, let it not be once named among you, as becometh saints; neither filthiness, nor foolish talking, nor jesting, which are not convenient; but rather giving of thanks" (Ephesians 5:3-4).

Thus, the "giving of thanks" is in contrast to the whole, black list that stands above. In Ephesians 5:20 it is even stronger: "Giving thanks always for all things unto God and the Father in the name of our Lord Jesus Christ." How inclusive are the "all things" for which we are to give thanks? These same "all things" are also mentioned in the book of Romans: "And we know that all things work together for good to them that love God, to them who are the called according to his purpose" (8:28). This is not a kind of magic— the infinite-personal God promises that he will work all things together for the Christian's good.

Here I am told that if I am a true Christian, "all things" work together for my good. It is not all things except the sorrow; it is not all things except the battle. We throw the words "all things" in Romans 8:28 around *all things*. We do honor to God and the finished work of Christ as we throw that circle around the whole; *all things* work together for good to those "who love God," for those "who are the called according to his purpose." But to the extent to which we properly throw the term "all things" around all things, it carries with it also the "all things" of Ephesians 5:20: "Giving thanks always for all things unto God and the Father. . . ." We cannot separate these two. The "all things" of Ephesians 5:20 is as wide as the "all things" of Romans 8:28. It must be giving of thanks for *all* things—this is God's standard.

Philippians deals with this also. In Philippians 4:6 we read, "Be careful for nothing; but in everything by prayer and supplication with thanksgiving let your requests be made known unto God."

"Be careful for nothing" here means: Do not be overcome by care in anything, by worry in anything, but rather "by prayer and supplication with thanksgiving let your requests be made known unto God." Of course, this is a statement concerning prayer in contrast to the worry, but at the same time it carries with it the direct command to thank God in the midst of the prayer for the "everything." Or we may note Colossians 2:7: "Rooted and built up in him, and stablished in the faith, as ye have been taught, abounding therein with thanksgiving." You will notice this is linked to the sixth verse: "As ye have therefore received Christ Jesus the Lord, so walk ye in him." What does it mean to walk in Christ? It is to be "rooted and built up in him, and established in the faith." (And there are many of us who think this is *by* faith; the *instrument* to do this is faith) "Abounding therein with thanksgiving"; the final note is on the thanksgiving.

Then we find in Colossians 3:15: "And let the peace of God rule in your hearts, to the which also ye are called in one body; and be ye thankful." And verse 17: "And whatsoever ye do in word or deed, do all in the name of the Lord Jesus, giving thanks to God and the Father by him." And again in Colossians 4:2: "Continue in prayer, and watch in the same with thanksgiving."

These words about thanksgiving are, in one sense, hard words. They are beautiful, but they do not give us any room to move—the "all things" includes *all things*.

We read in 1 Thessalonians 5:18: "In every thing give thanks: for this is the will of God in Christ Jesus concerning you." And this is linked to the next verse, verse 19: "Quench not the Spirit." Surely one thing is clear. God says to us: in *everything* give thanks.

I think we can see all this in its proper perspective if we go back to Romans 1:21: "Because that, when they knew God, they glorified him not as God, neither were thankful; but became vain in their imaginations, and their foolish heart was darkened." This is the central point: They were not thankful. Instead of giving thanks they "became vain in their imaginations, and their foolish heart was darkened." Professing themselves to be wise, they became fools. The beginning of man's rebellion against God was, and is, the lack of a thankful heart. They did not have proper, thankful hearts—seeing themselves as creatures before the Creator and being bowed not only in their knees, but in their stubborn hearts. The rebellion is a deliberate refusal to be the creature before the Creator, to the extent of being thankful. Love must carry with it a "thank-you," not in a superficial or "official" way, but in being thankful and saying in the mind or with the voice "Thank you" to God. As we shall see later, this is not to be confused with failing to stand against what is cruel in the world as it now is, but it *does* mean having a thankful heart toward the God who is there.

Two things are immediately involved here, if we are to see this in the Christian framework rather than in a non-Christian one. The first is that as Christians we say we live in a *personal universe,* in the sense that it was created by a personal God. Now that we have accepted Christ as our Savior, God the Father is our Father. When we say we live in a *personal universe* and God the Father is our Father, to the extent that we have less than a trusting attitude we are denying what we say we believe. We say that, as Christians, we have by choice taken the place of creatures before the Creator, but as we show a lack of trust, we are exhibiting that *at that moment,* in practice, we have not really so chosen.

The second thing we must comprehend in order to understand a contented heart in the Christian framework, rather than in a non-Christian one, is illustrated by Camus's dilemma in *The Plague*. As Christians we say we live in a *supernatural universe* and that there is a battle, since the fall of man, and that this battle is in both the seen world and the unseen world. This is what we say we believe; we insist on this against the naturalists and against the anti-supernaturalists. If we really believe this, first, we can be contented and yet fight evil, and second, surely it is God's right to put us as Christians where he judges best in the battle.

In a Christian understanding of contentment, we must see contentment in relation to these things. To summarize, there is a *personal* God. He is my Father since I have accepted Christ as my Savior. Then surely when I lack trust, I am denying what I say I believe. At the same time, I say there is a battle in the universe, and God *is* God. Then, if I lack trust, what I am really doing is denying in practice that he has a right, as my God, to use me where he wants in the spiritual battle that exists in the seen and the unseen world. The trust and contentment must be in the Christian framework, but in the proper framework the contentment is deeply important.

If the contentment goes and the giving of thanks goes, we are not loving God as we should, and proper desire has become coveting against God. This inward area is the first place of loss of true spirituality. The outward is always just a result of it.

The second test as to when proper desire becomes coveting is that we should love men enough not to envy, and this is not only envy for money; it is for everything. It can, for instance, be envy of his spiritual gifts. There is a simple test for this. Natural desires have become coveting against a fellow creature, one of our kind, a fellow man, when we have a mentality that would give us secret satisfaction at his misfortune. If a man has something, and he loses it, do we have an inward pleasure? A secret satisfaction at his loss? Do not speak too quickly and say it is never so, because you will make yourself a liar. We must all admit that even when we get on in our Christian life, even in these areas where we say we are longing for the church of Jesus Christ to be more alive in our generation, often we have this awful secret satisfaction at the loss of other men, even at the loss of brothers in Christ. Now if this mentality is upon me, in any way, then my natural desires have become coveting. I am inwardly coveting, and I am not loving men as I should.

Inward coveting—lack of love toward men—soon tends to spill over into the external world. It cannot be kept in the internal world completely.

This occurs in various degrees. When I have a wrong regret that others have what I do not possess, and this regret is allowed to grow, very quickly it comes to make me dislike the person himself. Surely we all have felt this. As the Holy Spirit makes us increasingly honest with ourselves, we must acknowledge that often we have a dislike of a person because we have had wrong desire toward something of his. More than this, if I would be happy if he were to lose something, the next step in the external world is moving either subtly or more openly to cause him to have the loss, either in lying about him, stealing from him, or whatever it may be.

In 1 Corinthians 10:23-24 I am told that my longing in love should be to seek for the other man's good and not just my own: "All things are lawful for me, but all things edify not. Let no man seek his own, but every man another's wealth." And the same is true in 1 Corinthians 13:4-5: "Charity suffereth long, and is kind; charity envieth not; charity vaunteth not itself, is not puffed up, doth not behave itself unseemly, seeketh not her own. . . ."

When we read these things and understand that failure in these areas is really coveting, a lack of love, every one of us must be upon his knees as Paul was upon his knees when he saw the commandment not to covet; it destroys any superficial view of the Christian life.

These are the areas of true spirituality. These are the areas of true Christian living. They are not basically external; they are internal, they are deep; they go down into the areas of our lives we like to hide from ourselves. The inward area is the first place of loss of true Christian life, of true spirituality, and the outward sinful act is the result. If we can only get hold of this—that the internal is the basic, the external is always merely the result—it will be a tremendous starting place.

However, true spirituality, the Christian life, is even one step beyond this. So far we have moved from the concept of a small, limited list of things to the whole Ten Commandments and the whole Law of Love. And then we have moved from the external to the internal. But in both of these cases we have dealt largely with that which is negative. But true spirituality, the Christian life, is deeper than even a profound concept of a proper negative. True spirituality, the true Christian life, is finally positive. We have touched on this in "Thou shalt love the Lord thy God with all thy heart, and with all thy soul, and with all thy mind," and "Thou shalt love thy neighbour as thyself" (Matthew 22:37, 39). But let us now especially emphasize that true spirituality, that true Christian life, is not even simply the proper negative in the deepest realms of our being. There is a biblical negative and then a positive.

As this study goes on, we shall deal more extensively with the following passages, but let us look at them quickly at this stage. Romans 6:4 is a biblical negative (and the tenses I read are the tenses as they are in Greek rather than the way they are translated in our King James translation): "Therefore we were buried with him by baptism into death." This is a negative. We were buried with him by baptism into death. We find the same thing in the first part of the sixth verse: "Knowing this, that our old man was crucified with him." When I accepted Christ as Savior, when God as Judge declared me justified, these things became legally true. My call in the Christian life is to see them become true in my life in practice. In Galatians 2:20 we find the same thing with a negative emphasis: "I have been crucified with Christ."

These negatives must never be overlooked, either in justification or the Christian life, or we will not be able to understand the following positives. In Galatians 6:14 we have this word: "But God forbid that I should glory, save in the cross of our Lord Jesus Christ, by whom [or whereby] the world is crucified unto me, and I unto the world." This is a tremendously strong negative. And this is not to be just a theoretical proposition; it is to be (as we shall see later) practiced, by the grace of God. There is a place, therefore, for a true biblical negative. But now let us go on and notice that the Christian life, true spirituality, does not stop with this negative. There is a positive.

So in Galatians 2:20 again, "I am crucified with Christ." Then there comes a break in the verse. In my own Bible I have marked it with two little lines, so that the break would be strongly apparent to me, even in a quick reading: "I have been crucified with Christ: [break] nevertheless I live; yet not I, but Christ liveth in me: and the life which I now live in the flesh I live by the faith of the Son of God, who loved me, and gave himself for me." So although there is a negative, it swept over into a positive, and to stop at the negative is to miss the whole point. The true Christian life is not an external life, or thought-life, of basic negatives; it is not hating life, in the way that we are apt to do when we get into despondency or other psychological problems. The Christian negative is not a nihilist negative—there is a true biblical negative—but the Christian life does not stop with a negative. There is a true life in the present as well as in the future.

In the book of Romans we feel the same force (6:4): "Therefore we were buried with him by baptism into death; that like as Christ was raised up from the dead by the glory of the Father, even so we also should walk in newness of life." This is the way it should be read: that "we *may* walk in newness of life." This is it; there is a positive. There is a possibility of walking in newness of life in the present life, right now, between the new birth and our death, or the second coming of Jesus. In Romans 6:6 it is the same: "Knowing this, that our old man was crucified with him, in order that the body of sin might be destroyed, that henceforth we should not serve sin." So we died with Christ, but we rose with Christ. That is the emphasis. Christ's death is a historic fact in the past, and we will be raised from the dead in future history, but there is to be a positive exhibition in present history, now, before our future resurrection. As an illustration, we read the negative in Galatians 5:15: "But if ye bite and devour one another, take heed that ye be not consumed one of another." He is talking of Christians. This is a negative. But there is a positive (verse 14): "For all the law is fulfilled in one word, even in this; Thou shalt love thy neighbour as thyself." And there is also a positive in verses 22 and 23 of the same chapter: "But the fruit of the Spirit is love, joy, peace, longsuffering, gentleness, goodness, faith, meekness, temperance: against such there is no law." So the context leads us from the negative to the positive in our considerations of the Christian life.

In summary then, of this chapter, which is an introduction to all that follows:

1. The true Christian life, true spirituality, does not *just* mean that we have been born again. It must begin there, but it means much more than that. It does not mean only that we are going to be in heaven. It does mean that, but it means much more than that. The true Christian life, true spirituality in the present life, means more than being justified and knowing that I am going to heaven.

2. It is not just a desire to get rid of taboos in order to live an easier and a looser life. Our desire must be for a deeper life. And when I begin to think of this, the Bible presents to me the whole of the Ten Commandments and the whole of the Law of Love.

3. True spirituality, the true Christian life, is not just outward, but it is inward—it is not to covet against God and men.

4. But it is even more than this: it is positive—positive in inward reality, and then positive in outward results. The inward thing is to be positive and not just negative; and then sweeping out of the inward

positive reality, there is to be a positive manifestation externally. It is not just that we are dead to certain things, but we are to love God, we are to be alive to him, we are to be in communion with him, *in this present moment of history*. And we are to love men, to be alive to men as men, and to be in communication on a true personal level with men, *in this present moment of history*.

When I speak of the Christian life, or freedom from the bonds of sin, or of true spirituality, the four points listed above are what the Bible says we should mean, and anything less than this is trifling with God—trifling with him who created the world, and trifling also with him who died on the cross. This is what we are to have in mind when we begin such a study; otherwise, there is no use even beginning to talk about experiential freedom from the bonds of sin or about an experiential reality of the Christian life, of true spirituality. If this is not in our minds, at least in some poor comprehension and at least in some poor aspiration, we might as well stop. Anything else is trifling with God, and because it is trifling with God, it is sin.

CHAPTER 2

THE CENTRALITY
OF DEATH

Now we begin the first of three closely related chapters in which we discuss *the basic considerations of the Christian life, or true spirituality*. We have already referred to a negative and a positive aspect of the Christian life. We will return now to the negative considerations. These negative considerations can be summed up in the words of four Bible verses:

- ☐ **Romans 6:4:** "We were buried with him by baptism into death."
- ☐ **Romans 6:6:** "Knowing this, that our old man was crucified with him."
- ☐ **Galatians 2:20:** "I am crucified with Christ."
- ☐ **Galatians 6:14:** "But God forbid that I should glory, save in the cross of our Lord Jesus Christ, by whom" [or whereby] "the world is crucified unto me, and I unto the world."

In these statements we find that as Christians we died, in God's sight, with Christ when we accepted him as Savior; but there is more to it than this. There is also very much the demand that in practice we are to die daily. That is the negative aspect that we mentioned in chapter 1 and that we will now pursue further.

As we said there, the Bible gives us a very sharp negative indeed—one that cannot be made an abstraction but that cuts into the hard stuff of normal life. We saw that the Word of God is definite that in all things, including hard things, we are to be contented, to say "Thank you" to God. Here is a negative, and it really is a negative; it is a negative of saying no toward the dominance of things and of self.

We also see that the Bible tells us that we are to love men, not only in a romantic or an idealized sense, but enough not to envy. Here again it would be false not to point out that this is a meaningless word, a pure romantic word; it is a pure utopian word in the bad sense, unless we see that this also involves a very strong negative aspect. If we have this right attitude, it means that we are saying no in certain very definite areas to certain things, and saying no to ourselves.

Again we must say this is not just something to be taken romantically, to stir up some sort of an emotion within ourselves. It is a very strong negative word. We are to be willing to say no to ourselves, we are to be willing to say no to things, in order that the command to love God and men may have real meaning. Even in things that are lawful to me, things that do not break the Ten Commandments, I am not to seek my own, but I am to seek another man's good. Now anyone who is thinking along honestly must say at this particular point that this seems like a hard position that is presented to us in Scripture. When we stand in the circle of mankind's usual perspective of life, and honestly face these things in the Bible, we must say one of two things. Either we must romanticize, and claim that these statements are intended just to give a good feeling, and some day, way off, in the reign of Christ in the future, or in the eternal heaven, it will mean something in practice. Or, if we do not say this, but face in a real sense these words as the Bible gives them, we must feel that we are against a hard wall. You cannot listen to this type of verse, this negative thrust in the Word of God concerning the Christian life, in a comfortable way, unless you romanticize it. Surely this has always been so, since the fall of man. But surely also it is *especially* so in the things-mentality and the success-mentality of the twentieth century. We are surrounded by a world that says no to nothing. When we are surrounded with this sort of mentality, in which everything is judged by binges and by success, then suddenly to be told that in the Christian life there is to be this strong negative aspect of saying no to things and no to self, it must seem hard. And if it does not feel hard to us, we are not really letting it speak to us.

In our culture we are often told that we should not say no to our children. Indeed, in our society repression is often correlated with evil. We have a society that holds itself back from nothing, except perhaps to gain something more in a different area. Any concept of a real no is avoided as much as possible. We who are a bit older may feel that we can say this *is* the younger generation. Much of the younger generation surely is like this: they know nothing of saying no to themselves or anything else. But this is only half true, because the older ones are also like this. The present mature generation has produced this environment, an environment of things and of success. We have produced a mentality of abundance, wherein everything is to be judged on the basis of whether it leads to abundance. Everything else must

FRANCIS SCHAEFFER

give in to this. Absolutes of any kind, ethical principles—everything must give in to affluence and selfish personal peace.

Of course this environment of not saying no fits exactly into our individual natural disposition, because, since the fall of man, we do not want to deny ourselves. Actually we do everything we can, whether it is in a philosophic sense or a practical sense, to put ourselves at the center of the universe. This is where we naturally want to live. And this natural disposition fits in exactly with the environment that surrounds us in the twentieth century.

This was the very crux of the Fall. When Satan said to Eve, "You shall not surely die . . . but you shall be like God," she *wanted* to be like God (Genesis 3:4-5). She did not want to say no to the fruit that was good to the eyes, even though God had told her to say no and had warned her of the consequences—and all the rest flowed from this. She put herself at the center of the universe; she wanted to be like God.

As I begin the Christian life I must face the fact with honesty. I must realize that there is, even for the Christian, an echoing equal wavelength within him with that which is all about him, where things and success are concerned. Consequently, it is false not to feel as if I were smashing against a strong wall when I consider this negative; it means I am fooling myself, I am not being honest. If I stand in the normal perspective of fallen man—and especially the normal perspective of the twentieth century—it is very hard indeed. But if I shift my perspective, the whole thing changes, and that is what I want to try in this second chapter—to begin to shift our perspective.

With this in mind, consider Luke 9:20-23, 27-31, 35:

> *He said unto them, But whom say ye that I am? Peter answering said, The Christ of God. And he straitly charged them, and commanded them to tell no man that thing; saying, The Son of man must suffer many things, and be rejected of the elders and chief priests and scribes, and be slain, and be raised the third day. And he said to them all, If any man will come after me, let him deny himself, and take up his cross daily, and follow me. . . . But I tell you of a truth, there be some standing here, which shall not taste of death, till they see the kingdom of God. And it came to pass about an eight days after these sayings, he took Peter and John and James, and went up into a mountain to pray. And as he prayed, the fashion of his countenance was altered, and his raiment was white and*

glistering. And, behold, there talked with him two men, which were Moses and Elias: who appeared in glory, and spake of his decease which he should accomplish at Jerusalem. . . . And there came a voice out of the cloud, saying, This is my beloved Son: hear him.

"And he said to them all, If any man will come after me, let him deny [or renounce] himself" (verse 23). That is the same thing we read in Corinthians—not seeking our own "things" even if we have rights to them.

"Who appeared in glory, and spake of his decease"—and this word "spake" in the Greek has a sense of continuing to speak; it is not just one short speaking. It is a *continuing* to speak of Christ's coming death that is involved here.

Luke 9:35 puts us in a different perspective: "This is my Son: listen to him!" We have here at the Mount of Transfiguration a preview of Christ in his glory. We have here a preview of that portion of the kingdom of God in which we stand after we have accepted Christ as our Savior. But we are swept on beyond this to the Resurrection, not only Christ's resurrection, but our future resurrection; we are swept on to the reign of Christ, and to eternity.

This is a different perspective. It is a perspective that is completely the antithesis of the world's perspective, which normally surrounds us. When we begin to look at these words in this setting, this totally other perspective—the perspective of the kingdom of God rather than the perspective of the fallen world and our own fallen nature—it is different. Pressure is put upon us by a world that does not want to say no to self—not just for a minor reason, but out of principle, because they are determined to be the center of the universe. When we step out of that very black perspective and into the perspective of the kingdom of God, then these negatives that are laid upon us take on an entirely different aspect.

You notice that they *kept speaking* of Christ's coming death. It was the topic of conversation. We are not told how long they talked, but it was not the speaking of a single phrase, it was a conversation that continued; they spoke, *kept speaking,* of his coming death. Remember that when John the Baptist introduced Jesus Christ, he said, "Behold the Lamb of God" (John 1:29). As he introduced Jesus Christ, he directed consideration to Christ's death. Here on the Mount of Transfiguration, in this environment of the kingdom of God, the conversation was involved with an extended talk about Christ's coming death.

Here then is the wonder of wonders, the wonder of the ages. Here is true perspective, in which the conversation is centered on one topic: The person who is God was to die. This one is the one who is referred to in verse 35: "This is my beloved Son: hear him." Moses and Elijah *kept speaking* of "his decease which he should accomplish at Jerusalem" (verse 31). Here God, as a true man after the Incarnation, comes as the Lamb of God to take away the sin of the world. It is not a false line in our poetry when we say: "Christ, the mighty Maker, died."

Now let us think of this situation, in considering the question of true perspective. Let us notice that this is the very center of the Christian message. Its center is not Christ's life, nor his miracles, but his *death*. The whole liberal theology today, seeing the problem of man as metaphysical, would put the solution in the concept of an incarnation. Not that they believe in a true incarnation, but they accept the *concept* of incarnation. But this is not the scriptural place of answer. The Nativity is the necessary thing to open the way for the answer, but the answer itself is the death of the Lord Jesus Christ. In Genesis 3:15, where the first promise of the coming of the Messiah was given, we are told that the Messiah, when he comes, shall be bruised. He shall crush Satan, but he shall be bruised in the process. In Genesis 3:21, how is man to be clothed now that he has sinned? With skins, requiring the shedding of blood. In Genesis 22 we read about the great event which shows Abraham's comprehension concerning the Messiah who was to come. His son must be placed upon the altar, as a sacrifice—and then a ram is supplied, thus giving a double picture of substitution. In Exodus 12, in the Passover (looking forward to the coming of Jesus), the Passover lamb died. In Isaiah 53, this great prophecy made seven hundred years before Jesus came, what is the center of the matter? It is words like these: "wounded," "bruised," "a lamb to the slaughter," "cut off out of the land of the living," "poured out his soul unto death." These words roll down through the centuries in prophecy, and we come to John the Baptist, who speaks these words: "Behold the Lamb of God, which taketh away the sin of the world" (1:29). His death is the subject of thousands of years of prophecy. The center of the Christian message is the redemptive death of Jesus Christ.

Jesus Christ himself places the same center when, in John 3, speaking to Nicodemus, he says, "And as Moses lifted up the serpent in the wilderness, even so must the Son of man be lifted up" (v. 14). If this is compared with John 12:32-33, it will be seen that it refers specifically to Christ's coming death.

*For all have sinned, and come short of the glory of God; being justi-
fied freely by his grace through the redemption that is in Christ
Jesus: whom God hath set forth to be a propitiation through faith in
his blood, to declare his righteousness for the remission of sins that
are past, through the forebearance of God; to declare, I say, at this
time his righteousness: that he might be just, and the justifier of
him which believeth in Jesus. (Romans 3:23-26)*

*Who needeth not daily, as those high priests, to offer up sacrifice,
first for his own sins, and then for the people's: for this he did once,
when he offered up himself. (Hebrews 7:27)*

Turn where you will, it is the same. In the last book of the Bible, the
book of Revelation, we have the exclamation point to this in chapter 5, verse
9, where it speaks of the book of redemption: "And they sung a new song,
saying, Thou art worthy to take the book, and to open the seals thereof: for
thou wast slain, and hast redeemed us to God by thy blood out of every kin-
dred, and tongue, and people, and nation."

If you turn to the theology of the early church (and never make the
mistake of thinking that the early church did not have a theology), the
substitutionary death of Christ is equally the center.

What is central in the Christian message of good news, the Evangel to
the world? It centers in only one thing—the redemptive death of the Lord
Jesus Christ.

From the time of the Fall, and the first promise within twenty four
hours after the Fall took place, until the very end, this is the message.

So we are not to be surprised that Elijah and Moses, meeting with
Jesus on the Mount of Transfiguration, had this as their key topic of conversation. "And, behold, there talked with him two men, which were Moses
and Elias: who appeared in glory, and spake [and continued to speak] of his
decease which he should accomplish at Jerusalem" (Luke 9:30-31). Of
course they talked about it, because they had a stake in this. It was important
for them not merely as a theological proposition, but the salvation of Moses
and Elijah rested upon this single point—the coming death of Jesus on Calvary's cross. The disciples who were there that day had a stake in this, too,
because if Jesus had not died upon the cross, they too would have had no
salvation. And let us say to each one who reads this: We have a stake in this,
for there is no salvation possible to us unless Jesus died on Calvary's cross.

Now the death of the Lord Jesus is absolutely unique. It is substitutionary. There is no death like Jesus' death. There is no parallel death to Jesus' death—this must stand as absolute in our thinking. His substitutionary death on the cross, in space and time in history, had infinite value because of who he is as God. Thus nothing need be added to the substitutionary value of his death, nor can anything be added. He died once for all. Having said that as forcefully as we can state it, we add that, nevertheless, in Luke 9:22-24, we find Christ puts forth a chronological order. In verse 22: "The Son of man must suffer many things, and be rejected of the elders and chief priests and scribes, and be slain, and be raised the third day." The order is in three steps: rejected, slain, raised. This speaks of his coming unique and substitutionary death, yet this *order*—rejected, slain, raised—is immediately related by Jesus Christ himself, in verses 23 and 24, to us, the Christians. "And he said unto them all, If any man will come after me, let him deny himself [renounce himself], and take up his cross daily, and follow me. For whosoever will save his life shall lose it: but whosoever will lose his life for my sake, the same shall save it." Here Jesus takes this order that was so necessary for our redemption in the unique substitutionary death of the Lord Jesus Christ and applies it to the Christian's life. The order—rejected, slain, raised—is also the order of the Christian life of true spirituality; there is no other.

If we forget the absolute uniqueness of Christ's death, we are in heresy. As soon as we set aside or minimize, as soon as we cut down in any way, as the liberals of all kinds do in their theology, on the uniqueness and substitutionary character of Christ's death, our teaching is no longer Christian. On the other hand, let us remember the other side of this matter. If we forget the relationship of this order to us as Christians, then we have a sterile orthodoxy, and we have no true Christian life. Christian life will wither and die; spirituality in any true biblical sense will come to an end.

Jesus is talking here about our death by choice in the present life. He applies it to a specific situation to make it most concrete. In verse 26: "For whosoever shall be ashamed of me and my words, of him shall the Son of man be ashamed, when he shall come in his own glory, and in his Father's, and of the holy angels." The Bible is not speaking of some romantic feeling, some idealization, some abstraction. Jesus carries this concept of facing the rejection, being slain, down into a very practical situation: facing an alien world. It is the saying no to self when our natural selves would desire acceptance by the alien world—a world in revolt against its Creator and our Lord.

As we look in the New Testament as a whole, we find that this command of Christ is not limited to one situation, it is that which is to be the whole mentality and outlook of the Christian's life. What is being presented to us here is the question of the Christian's mentality in all of life, and the order stands: rejected, slain, raised. As Christ's rejection and death are the first steps in the order of redemption, so our rejection and death to things and self are the first steps in the order of true and growing spirituality. As there could be no next step in the order of Christ's redemption until the step of death was taken, so in the Christian there can be no further step until these first two steps are faced—not in theory only, but at least in some practical practice. Rejected, slain.

How central was Christ's death for our redemption? See Moses and Elijah standing there on the Mount of Transfiguration with Christ, all talking about this, discussing at length his coming death. They *kept speaking* about it. Equally it can be said how central and fundamental is our individual and continuing death by choice as Christians.

The death was central to the work of Christ and therefore it provoked conversation; the prophets spoke of it in the Old Testament, and Moses, Elijah, and Christ conversed about it in the New. In the Christian life, it is just as central, and should it not provoke continuing thought, continuing consideration and conversation, and continuing prayer on our part? So I must ask, very gently: How much thought does the necessity of death by choice provoke, how much conversation? How much prayer does this provoke for ourselves and for those we love? Is it not true that our thoughts, our prayers for ourselves and those we love, and our conversations are almost entirely aimed at getting rid of the negative at any cost—rather than praying that the negatives might be faced in the proper attitude? How much prayer do we make for our children and those we love that they may indeed be willing to walk, by the grace of God, through the steps of rejection and being slain? We are infiltrated by the world with its attitudes, rather than the attitudes of the perspective of the kingdom of God. Not that we should live only in the negative, as we shall see as we go on in this series of studies, nevertheless it is important that we have an understanding of the order. We must not think we can rush on to the last step without the reality of being rejected and slain, not just at that point in our lives when we become Christians but as a continuing situation in our lives.

With this new perspective of the kingdom of God, let us look at the negative aspects of the Ten Commandments in Exodus 20.

In the first commandment is set forth a call to say a strong negative toward wanting to be in the place of God. This is the key to the whole thing: wanting to be in the center of the universe. We are, by choice, to die to this.

The rest of the commandments show the same thing, as we have them set out in Exodus chapter 20. We are, by choice, to die to the time God has kept for himself, his special day. We are to say a strong negative toward grasping any authority that is not properly our own. We are, by choice, to say no to personally taking human life. We are to reject the concept of taking any sexual things which are not rightfully ours. And we are to say no to marring, by false accusation, reputations that are not ours.

The last commandment, "Thou shalt not covet," shows that these negatives are related not just to outward behavior, but also to inward attitudes. Here is our death, in reality. But when is that death to be died? Certainly not after such a long delay that our physical bodies have lost their desire and zest for things. We are to say no by choice—to die to self—at the point when we are in the midst of a living, moving life that could want the things and find enjoyment in them. This "death" is not to be pushed out or pushed back, nor is it to be related only to the moment of physical death. We can indeed say that we shall be perfect when Jesus comes, when he raises us from the dead, but that is not the point at issue here. Here, in the midst of life, where there is battle and strife, there is to be a strong negative, by choice and by the grace of God. It is not, for example, a matter of waiting until we no longer have strong sexual desires, but rather that in the midst of the moving of life, surrounded by a world that grabs everything in rebellion, first against God and then against fellow men, we are to understand what Jesus means when he talks about denying ourselves and renouncing ourselves with regard to that which is not rightfully ours.

There will be some pain here. Indeed, there are splinters in the Christian's cross as we are surrounded in this present life by an atmosphere alien to the kingdom of God. But this is the way of the Cross: "The Son of man must suffer many things, and be rejected of the elders and chief priests and scribes, and be slain, and be raised the third day" (Luke 9:22). We can see how the order of events has meaning for us as Christians after justification: rejected, slain, raised. Here the reference is to rejection specifically by the religious leaders of his day—men who had taken the world's way instead of God's. But at heart it is rejection by the world itself, and this rejection must precede any possibility of knowing anything about the risen life.

We see further that this rejection is not a once-for-all thing. Christ called his followers to take up the cross *daily*. True, we accept Christ as Savior once for all; we are justified and our guilt is gone forever. But after that there is this daily, moment-by-moment aspect. The existentialist is right when he puts his emphasis on the reality of the moment-by-moment situation. He is wrong in many things, but he is right here.

In Luke 14:27 Jesus says a similar thing: "And whosoever doth not bear his cross, and come after me, cannot be my disciple." He is not saying that a man cannot be saved without this, but that you are not Christ's disciple, in the sense of following him, if this is not your way of life: rejected and slain—daily! And he puts the command not in an abstract but in an intensely practical setting, in verse 26 relating it to his followers' fathers, mothers, wives, children, brothers, sisters, and their own lives. He sets it among the realities of daily life. This is where we must die.

"For which of you, intending to build a tower, sitteth not down first, and counteth the cost, whether he have sufficient to finish it? Lest haply, after he hath laid the foundation, and is not able to finish it, all that behold it begin to mock him, saying, This man began to build, and was not able to finish" (Luke 14:28-30). This is a unit with what has gone before, a unit tied together by Jesus himself. "Count the cost," he says. And surely, in our preaching to lost man, we must emphasize the fact that part of being a Christian is the element of bearing one's cross daily. We are in an alien world built upon man's rebellion against God, and in this life the Christian himself is not yet totally free from elements of this rebellion within himself.

As I have said, Romans 6 begins with many strong negatives, and though we may want to rush on to the second half of verse 4 ("As Christ was raised up from the dead . . . even so we also should walk in newness of life"), actually we are in peril if we ignore the element of "dying." "Buried with him by baptism unto death," "dead to sin," "baptized into his death": the way into the freedom of the second part of verse 4 is through these, not around them. The order is absolute: rejected, slain, raised. It is the same in verse 6 of the same chapter. We must walk through the first half ("Knowing this, that our old man is crucified with him") before we can get on to the second half ("That the body of sin might be destroyed, that henceforth we should not serve sin.") I think I perceive that most Christians even read the first half of these verses faster, in order to get to the second, "happy" part of the verses, but this is a mistake. We love to skip along, but one does not get on the other side of a door without going through it, and we do not get to the joyous second part of these verses without passing through the first part.

This is, first of all, true absolutely and once for all at justification, but then it is true moment by moment in practice in the Christian life. Let us not be confused here. The moment we accepted Jesus Christ as our Savior, we were justified and our guilt was gone once for all. That is absolute. But if we want to know anything of reality in the Christian life, anything of true spirituality, we must "take up our cross daily." The principle of saying no to self lies at the heart of my attitude toward the world as it maintains its alien stand in rebellion against the Creator. If I use my intellectual capacities to make myself respectable to the world, as it is in revolution against the one who created it, then I have failed. It is equally true if I use my ignorance for the same purpose. I am to face the cross of Christ in every part of life and with my whole man. The cross of Christ is to be a reality to me not only once for all at my conversion, but all through my life as a Christian. True spirituality does not stop at the negative, but without the negative—in comprehension and practice—we are not ready to go on.

CHAPTER 3

THROUGH DEATH
TO RESURRECTION

If this book were being set to music, this would be the moment for trumpets. We have been considering the importance of giving due weight to the negatives of the Christian life: rejected, slain. But now we turn to the positive, without which the other two can never represent a true, balanced spirituality: raised.

> *"Therefore we are buried with him by baptism into death: that like as Christ was raised up from the dead by the glory of the Father, even so we also should walk in newness of life" (Romans 6:4).*
>
> *"I have been crucified with Christ, nevertheless I live; yet not I, but Christ liveth in me: and the life which I now live in the flesh I live by the faith of the Son of God, who loved me, and gave himself for me" (Galatians 2:20).*

After the rejection of self, after the death to self, there is, and there continues to be, a resurrection.

The transfiguration of Christ expresses all this vividly. It was a prefiguration of Christ's resurrection, a time of glory. "As he prayed, the fashion of his countenance was altered, and his raiment was white and glistering" (Luke 9:29), or, as Matthew records it, "His face did shine as the sun, and his raiment was white as the light" (Matthew 17:2).

Now let me emphasize: these things happened in history. This is important, especially today, when religious things are constantly being pushed away into a nonhistoric realm of an "other." But here, in the account of the Transfiguration, we have an emphasis on time and space. Luke, for example, records that "on the next day, when they were come down from the hill, much people met him" (9:37). Christ and the disciples at a certain point in time went up the mountain, and at another point they came down. As they went up the hillside, they did not move into a nonspatial philosophical or religious "other." They were still connected in space with the foot of the mountain, and down there in the plain the normal activities of life were going on.

The same thing is true in the realm of time. Had they been wearing watches, the watches would not have stopped as they ascended the mountain and restarted as they came down again. Time was still going on, and when they came down, time had passed—it was the next day. History is made up of time and space: it is its warp and woof. And here on the Mount of Transfiguration true history took place, rooted in normal space and normal time. The glorification of Jesus was not in the world of the philosophical "other," or "upper-story," but in the hard realities of space and time, and the transfiguration demonstrates the hard reality of the words Jesus himself spoke as they came down from the hill: "The Son of man must suffer many things, and be rejected of the elders and chief priests and scribes, and be slain, and be raised the third day" (9:22). There it is: rejected, slain, raised in history.

When we come to the actual resurrection of Jesus Christ after his crucifixion, we find the same emphasis. He asked the disciples whom he met on the Emmaus road, "Ought not Christ to have suffered these things, and to enter into his glory?" (Luke 24:26). He asked the question on a certain day in the calendar, at a certain hour of the day, on a certain road on the map, rooting the event in space-time history. And he did this with all of his resurrection appearances. He "stood in the midst of them," in their normal, everyday life. In their fear they tried to push him off into another realm—"They were terrified . . . and supposed that they had seen a spirit"—but Jesus would not allow this. "Behold my hands and my feet, that it is I myself: handle me, and see; for a spirit hath not flesh and bones, as ye see me have" (Luke 24:37, 39). And then he took a piece of broiled fish and honeycomb, and "did eat before them" (v. 43), and he showed them his wounds, the marks of his death.

It was the same body, raised and glorified; not in some far-off place, but *there,* in space, time, and history.

In John 20 there is the same kind of an emphasis; it is not just an incidental repetition, but the center of the whole thing.

Then the same day at evening, being the first day of the week, when the doors were shut where the disciples were assembled for fear of

the Jews, came Jesus and stood in the midst, and said unto them,
Peace be unto you. (John 20:19)

Christ's body is changed, he can suddenly come through the locked doors, but that does not make any difference in that of which we are speaking. While it is true that he can come through the locked door, it is still the same body.

> *But Thomas, one of the twelve, called Didymus, was not with them*
> *when Jesus came. The other disciples therefore said unto him, We*
> *have seen the Lord. But he said unto them, Except I shall see in his*
> *hands the print of the nails, and put my finger into the print of the*
> *nails, and thrust my hand into his side, I will not believe. And after*
> *eight days again* [that is, a full week] *his disciples were within, and*
> *Thomas with them: then came Jesus, the doors being shut, and*
> *stood in the midst, and said, Peace be unto you. Then saith he to*
> *Thomas, Reach hither thy finger, and behold my hands; and reach*
> *hither thy hand, and thrust it into my side: and be not faithless, but*
> *believing. And Thomas answered and said unto him, My Lord and*
> *my God. (John 20:24-28)*

Let us notice that it is the same body. The locked doors do not shut him out, and he can appear in the midst, *but that makes no difference.* It is a body that can be touched and handled. In John 21:9 the emphasis is upon the eating: "As soon then as they were come to land, they saw a fire of coals there, and fish laid thereon, and bread."

Here we have the body of Jesus Christ in an external space-time world. The reality of the resurrection is not something to push off into a strange dimension. It is meaningful in our normal dimension.

> *To whom also he showed himself alive after his passion by many*
> *infallible* [space-time] *proofs, being seen of them forty days, and*
> *speaking of the things pertaining to the kingdom of God. (Acts 1:3)*

For forty days—not just a wisp, as it were—but for forty days, infallible proof was given.

Neither let us draw back from the great act of the Ascension: "And when he had spoken these things, while they beheld, he was taken up; and a cloud received him out of their sight" (Acts 1:9). This is the thing that, above every other, modern man cannot accept. The neoorthodox theologian may speak of a physical resurrection at times, but he will never speak of a physical ascension. When you come to material like John Robinson's book *Honest to God*, this is the place where the battle is pitched. *And it is the proper place to pitch it,* because here is a resurrected body that can eat, that can go up into heaven, and that can disappear into the cloud. We must remember at this point that Christ has been appearing and disappearing for forty days. The supernatural is not in one direction, as it were; he is here—he *was* here, rather—and then appeared again. Now something else is given to us that is real; again there is an emphasis on history, that the resurrected body of Jesus Christ did ascend into the clouds. It was at an hour of the day, on a day of the calendar. There was a moment when his feet left the Mount of Olives. Let us not draw back from this point. People who think that they can draw back from the physical ascension of Jesus and still maintain Christianity cannot be consistent in the rest of their position.

However, the space-timeness does not end there. Later in the book of Acts, we have Christ meeting Paul: "And as he journeyed [that is, Saul—later Paul], he came near Damascus: and suddenly there shined round about him a light from heaven: and he fell to the earth" (9:3-4). Notice here the connection with what we have already seen in the descriptive phrases that are connected with the Mount of Transfiguration:

> *Light shone round about him, and he fell to the earth, and heard a voice saying unto him, Saul, Saul, why persecutest thou me? And he said, Who art thou, Lord? And the Lord said, I am Jesus whom thou persecutest: it is hard for thee to kick against the pricks. And he trembling and astonished said, Lord, what wilt thou have me to do? And the Lord said unto him, Arise, and go into the city, and it shall be told thee what thou must do. And the men which journeyed with him stood speechless, hearing a voice, but seeing no man. And Saul arose from the earth; and when his eyes were opened, he saw no man: but they led him by the hand, and brought him into Damascus. (9:3-9)*

He had been made blind by the glory-light. Where? On the road to Damascus. So definitely is the space-situation fixed. And the time could be told. There was an hour of the day when this took place.

The same thing is repeated in Acts 22:6: "And it came to pass, that, as I made my journey, and was come nigh unto Damasus about noon, [there is a space-element, the road to Damascus; there is a time-element, very close to noon] suddenly there shone from heaven a great light round about me." And the eleventh verse: "And when I could not see for the glory of that light, [that is why he was blinded: it was not just some mystical thing, but the sheer glory of the light which made him blind for a time] being led by the hand of them that were with me, I came into Damascus."

In chapter 26 the story is repeated again, with a very significant addition: "At midday, O king, I saw in the way a light from heaven, above the brightness of the sun" (verse 13). Here is the first addition: it was at midday; nevertheless, at the brightest hour of the Near Eastern sun, here was a brighter light, a light of the glorified Christ, "shining round about me and them which journeyed with me. And when we were all fallen to the earth, I heard a voice speaking unto me, and *saying in the Hebrew tongue . . .*" (verse 14, emphasis added).

This is one of the most significant things in the Word of God in the midst of twentieth-century discussion. Here is a declaration that you have space, time, history, and rational communication. The rational communication comes not through some mystical experience of Paul, but in the midst of space and time, the glorified Christ, the raised Christ, spoke to him *in terms of the Hebrew language.* At noon, on the road to Damascus, Jesus appeared—the glorified Christ in history—speaking in a normal language, using normal words and normal grammar, to a man named Saul. With this, there is a complete denial of the twentieth-century projection of these things into a religiously "other" world. Here we are in the realm of space, time, history, normal communication, and normal language.

But again, it does not stop here. Later, many years later, there was another man, named John. He was on the isle of Patmos. And the first chapter of the book of Revelation tells us that he sees Jesus again. And by "again," I mean after Paul had seen him. I am not saying this is the only other appearance—for example, Stephen also saw him—but here are two clear steps some time after the Ascension. After the Ascension, the glorified Christ was seen in space and in time on the Damascus road by Saul. After the Ascension, the glorified Christ was seen on the isle of Patmos—again, a spatial identification. The isle of Patmos is still there. Actually, there is not only a spatial identification: there is time, too. It was the Lord's Day.

31

And I turned to see the voice that spake with me. And being turned, I saw seven golden candlesticks; and in the midst of the seven candlesticks one like unto the Son of man, clothed with a garment down to the foot, and girt about the paps with a golden girdle. His head and his hairs were white like wool, as white as snow; and his eyes were as a flame of fire. (Revelation 1:12-14)

John is describing here what he actually saw. This is not strange, or incongruous, any more than it was when, after his resurrection, Christ's eating was spoken of in normal terms.

And his feet like unto fine brass, as if they burned in a furnace; and his voice as the sound of many waters. And he had in his right hand seven stars: and out of his mouth went a sharp twoedged sword: and his countenance was as the sun shineth in his strength. And when I saw him, I fell at his feet as dead. And he laid his right hand upon me, saying unto me, Fear not; I am the first and the last: I am he that liveth and was dead; and, behold, I am alive for evermore, Amen; and have the keys of hell and of death. (Revelation 1:15-18)

We are not told in what language he spoke, but it was human speech, of the same nature as that which Saul heard on the Damascus road. More than that, in this chapter, there is a careful delineation between what is actual description and what is to be understood as figures of speech.

Even this is not the end. The Bible tells us of the future coming of Jesus to the earth, and describes this visible coming in terms that have to do with space and time and history. This is future to us still, but it is nevertheless space-timeness:

And I saw heaven opened, and behold a white horse; and he that sat upon him was called Faithful and True, and in righteousness he doth judge and make war. His eyes were as a flame of fire, and on his head were many crowns; and he had a name written, that no man knew, but he himself. And he was clothed with a vesture dipped in blood: and his name is called The Word of God. And the armies which were in heaven followed him upon white horses, clothed in fine linen, white and clean. And out of his mouth goeth a sharp sword, that with it he should smite the nations: and he shall

rule them with a rod of iron: and he treadeth the winepress of the
fierceness and wrath of Almighty God. And he hath on his vesture
and on his thigh a name written, KING OF KINGS, AND LORD
OF LORDS. (Revelation 19:11-16)

Again there is a spaceness here, because we are told the place: Armageddon, that is, the mountain of Megiddo (Revelation 16:16). The place where he later comes and touches the earth is spoken of in the Old Testament: it is the Mount of Olives (Zechariah 14:4). At each point it is the same. The glory and wonder of Christ are not pushed off into a world that is "other" than our own. In each of these cases, intriguingly enough, there is identification of space, identification of time. There is a real, historic death of Jesus Christ. There is a real, historic Resurrection. And there is a real, historic future glorification that is meaningful in terms of space, time, and history: *our own* space, time, and history.

The Bible says that the day will come when both saved and unsaved men will look upon the glorified Christ. They will see him. Every man will see him, not as a religious idea, but glorified, in a real space-time situation. But these passages not only say that he will be so, but that he is so *now*. The glorification of the Lord Jesus Christ is not pushed off only into a future moment when he shall be seen by all men. It is not pushed off into that great moment when he shall come in glory and we are told every knee shall bow. He is glorified now. The Ascension was not a disappearance into a nothingness, into the world of mere religious ideas. Between his ascension from the Mount of Olives, and his appearance on the Damascus road he did not cease to be. And again there was not a great void into which he disappeared from the time of his appearance on the Damascus road until John saw him on the isle of Patmos. This is Jesus *as he is now*. He is so glorified, at this present moment.

As we contemplate these things, several things must immediately come before us. First of all, as we consider Jesus speaking in the Hebrew tongue on the Damascus road, and appearing to John and speaking to him on the isle of Patmos, we have here clear proof of a *historic* resurrection of Jesus Christ. But there is much more than this. This physical resurrection is the proof of the finished work of Jesus Christ on the cross, proof that the work is really done, that nothing need be added to his glorious substitutionary work for our justification.

But even this does not exhaust the matter. We are told in the Word of God, by the apostle Paul, that in Christ's resurrection we see the promise, the firstfruits, of our own coming physical resurrection. What we see him to be after his resurrection, Paul insists, *we shall be.* When I consider the resurrection of Jesus Christ, not merely in the world of religious ideas or ideals, but in the world of space and time and reality, I have the promise from the hand of God himself that I will be so raised from death. This body is so much of myself, in the total personality—the whole man—and it will not be left behind in the salvation that is brought forth through Jesus Christ. His death on the cross is of such a nature that the *whole man* will be redeemed. In one specific day, the Christian's body will be raised from death, like Christ's risen body, glorified.

But there is more even than this. The reality, the space-timeness of the physical resurrection of Jesus Christ means something to us also today: "What shall we say then? Shall we continue in sin that grace may abound?" (Romans 6:1). Paul is not talking about some far-off time, he is talking about the redeemed in the present circumstances.

> *What shall we say then? Shall we continue in sin that grace may abound? God forbid. How shall we, that are dead to sin, live any longer therein? Know ye not, that so many of us as were baptized into Jesus Christ were baptized into his death? Therefore we were buried with him by baptism into death; that like as Christ was raised up from the dead by the glory of the Father, even so we also should walk in newness of life. For if we have been planted together in the likeness of his death, we shall be also in the likeness of his resurrection: knowing this, that our old man is crucified with him, that the body of sin might be destroyed, that henceforth we should not serve sin. For he that is dead is freed from sin. Now, if we be dead with Christ, we believe we shall also live with him: knowing that Christ being raised from the dead dieth no more; death hath no more dominion over him. For in that he died, he died unto sin once: but in that he liveth, he liveth unto God. Likewise reckon ye also yourselves to be dead indeed unto sin, but alive unto God through Jesus Christ our Lord. Let not sin therefore reign in your mortal body, that ye should obey it in the lusts thereof. (Romans 6:1-12)*

Let us carefully notice some points here. First, Christ died in history. That is the point we have been making. He died in space, time, and history.

If you had been there that day, you could have taken your hand and rubbed it across the rough wood of the cross of Jesus Christ—you could have gotten a splinter in your hand from the cross.

Second, Christ rose in history, and we have made a strong point of this, too. Christ rose and he was glorified, *in history.*

This is the exact opposite of the liberal theology, which speaks of the *kerygma,* that we make Jesus the Christ *when we preach him.* Nothing could be further from the truth. It is a total denial of the wonder of the teaching of the Bible. We do not make Jesus the Christ when we preach him. Jesus *is* the Christ, whether we preach him or not. Men may not know the wonder of the gospel if we do not preach it, but our failure to preach cannot change the fact of the person or the glory of the Lord Jesus Christ. On this present day he is raised, he is glorified. If no one preached Jesus Christ today, and no one thought once even of the word "God," it would make no difference whatsoever to the fact that Jesus is the Christ. He rose in history, he is glorified now. And this word of his resurrection, of his present glory, has meaning in our present space-time world.

Third, we died with Christ when we accepted him as Savior. If I have accepted Christ as Savior, this is now a past thing in history. The individual Christian's salvation is rooted in two space-time historic points. The first is the finished work of Jesus on the cross of Calvary, and the second is the point of time when, by the grace of God, the individual accepted Jesus Christ as Savior. Here are two space-time points upon which our salvation rests. And if I have accepted Jesus as my Savior in the past, then Paul can speak concerning me: "Therefore being justified [in the past] by faith, we have [in the present] peace with God through our Lord Jesus Christ" (Romans 5:1). This is clearly the thrust of the whole statement, from the tenses of the Greek text.

In Romans 6:2, this is connected in this way: "God forbid. How shall we, that are dead [that is, died] to sin, live any longer therein?"

The verb "died" is in the aorist tense. When we accepted Christ as our Savior, in God's sight we died with Christ. "Therefore we are [that is, were] buried with him by baptism into death" (Romans 6:4). That refers to the time when we accepted Jesus as our Savior. "Knowing this, that our old man is [that is, was] crucified with him" (6:6). So here we have the third historic point. Christ died in history; Christ rose in history; we died with Christ when we accepted him as Savior. This, too, is a historic thing. It is something that happened (past tense) at a point of history.

The fourth point is that we will be raised by him as he was raised. And this will be a point of future history. The clock keeps going. And when the Christian is raised from death, the great trumpet sounds, the word is spoken and every Christian comes forth from the grave at the command of Jesus Christ; the clock on the wall will not stop, it will still turn. The clock is almost ready to strike three as I write this. It is conceivable that Jesus will come before five past. If such is the case, the clock on the wall will not stop turning. At ten past, the clock will still run on. This is the biblical picture. The future resurrection, with this present body, and our future changing will take place in a twinkling of an eye: in *history*, in space-time, true history.

> *For if we have been united with him in the likeness of his death, we shall be also in the likeness of his resurrection. (Romans 6:5)*

This truly refers to his resurrection, but "resurrection" is the emphasized thought. In the Greek, the "his" is left out; the emphasis is upon resurrection. "We shall be [future] in the likeness of resurrection."

> *Now if we died with Christ we believe we shall also live with him. (Romans 6:8)*

This is the future tense. We died with Christ when we accepted him as Savior *in history.* We will be raised physically or changed in the twinkling of an eye *in a moment of history.*

But that is not all. There is more here, a fifth point. These great truths are to be brought down into the area of present Christian life and true spirituality. The Bible says that in the present life we are, in practice, to live by faith *as though we are dead now.*

> *For in that he died, he died unto sin once for all: but in that he liveth he liveth unto God. Likewise reckon [this is an act of faith] ye also yourselves to be dead indeed unto sin. (Romans 6:10-11)*

As Jesus died in history, and once for all was dead to sin, so now we are called in faith to count ourselves dead, in practice, at this present moment of history; not in some far-off world of religious ideas, but in reality, at this moment on the clock. By faith we are to live now as though we have already died.

But even that is not all. If it were, it would include only the two words "rejected" and "slain." But the words are rejected, slain, *and raised*: raised, not just as an idea of future physical resurrection, though that will be real and future to every Christian, but as a present thing. So the sixth point is that we are to live by faith now, in the present history, as though we had been raised already from death. That is the message of the Christian life. That is the basic consideration we are discussing.

> *Therefore we are [were] buried with him by baptism into death: that like as Christ was raised up from the dead by the glory of the Father, even so we also should walk in newness of life.*
> *(Romans 6:4)*

Paul is not speaking here of the future millennium or eternity; that is a different thing altogether. It is *now:* We "should [may] walk in newness of life. . . . Knowing this, that our old man is [was] crucified with him, that the body of sin might be destroyed, that henceforth we should not serve sin" (Romans 6:6). How? By faith: "Likewise reckon ye also yourselves to be dead indeed unto sin, but alive unto God through Jesus Christ our Lord" (Romans 6:11).

When? Right now! This is the basic consideration of the Christian life. First, Christ died in history. Second, Christ rose in history. Third, we died with Christ in history, when we accepted him as our Savior. Fourth, we will be raised in history, when he comes again. Fifth, we are to live by faith now as though we were now dead, already have died. And sixth, we are to live now by faith as though we have now already been raised from the dead.

Now what does this mean in practice, so that it will not be just words going over our heads? First of all, it certainly means this: that in our thoughts and lives now we are to live *as though we had already died, been to heaven, and come back again as risen.*

Remember, at least one man has gone there and come back. Paul speaks of such a man in 2 Corinthians 12:2-4. I think it was Paul himself, but whether it was Paul or another, certainly there was such a man.

Paul writes, "I knew a man in Christ above fourteen years ago, (whether in the body I cannot tell; or whether out of the body, I cannot tell: God knoweth;) such an one was caught up to the third heaven." Paul is saying that this man went to heaven; he was caught up in the third heaven. The third heaven is used here in the sense of the presence of God. It does not necessarily mean far off, but the presence of God. The point is that this man was caught up into heaven, *and then he came back.*

Can't you imagine this man as he came back from heaven? He had seen it as a propositional truth, as a brute fact. He had been there, and looked at it, and then had come back. Would anything ever have looked the same to him again? It is as though he had died. It is as though he had been raised from the dead. Just as the Mount of Transfiguration gives us a different perspective when we are in the perspective of the kingdom of God, how different this man's perspective would have been all his life. The constant pressure to conform to the world about us, the social pressure and every other kind of pressure of our day—surely it would have been broken. How could he conform to this, which is so marred, so broken, so caught up in revolution against God, so disgusting? How *could* he, in comparison with what he had seen? What would the praise of the world be worth when one had stood in the presence of God? The wealth of the world, what would it look like beside the treasures of heaven? Man longs for power. But what is earthly power after one has seen the reality of heaven and the power of God? All things would look different. Surely all of this is involved in the statement that we are to live by faith now, as though we had already died, and already been raised from the dead.

But Romans 6 does not leave it here, as though we are merely projecting our imaginations. There is more to it than this. "For in that he died, he died unto sin once for all; but in that he liveth, he liveth unto God" (Romans 6:10). Jesus Christ lives indeed in the presence of the Father. This is where we are called to live. We are to be dead in this present life! Dead both to good and bad, in order to be alive to the presence of God. Yes, even to good. We are to be dead—not unconscious, not locked away in some darkness, but alive to God in communion with him, in communication with him. Our call to faith in this present life is that we should live as though dead to *all* things that we might be alive to God.

This is what it means now, as I wrote earlier, to love God enough to be contented, to love him enough in the present world to say thank you in all the ebb and flow of life. When I am dead both to good and bad, I have my face turned towards God. And this is the place in which, by faith at the present moment of history, I am to be. When I am there, what am I? I am then the creature in the presence of the Creator, acknowledging that he is my Creator, and I am only a creature, nothing more. It is as though I am already in the grave and already before the face of God.

But one more note needs to be sounded. We must not stop here!

When through faith I am dead to all, and am face-to-face with God, then I am ready by faith to *come back into this present world*, as though I have already been raised from the dead. It is as though I anticipate that day when I *will* come back. I will be in that number, as will all who have accepted Jesus as Savior, when the heavens open and we come back, following Jesus Christ in our resurrected, glorified bodies. And so now I am ready to come back as though back from the grave, as though the resurrection had already taken place, and step back into this present historic, space-time world. "Likewise reckon ye also yourselves to be dead indeed unto sin, [that is where I stopped before, but it does not stop there] but alive unto God through Jesus Christ our Lord" (Romans 6:11).

Neither yield [here is the faith] *ye your members* [that is, in the present world] *as instruments* [weapons, arms, tools] *of unrighteousness unto sin: but yield yourselves unto God, as those that are alive* [right now] *from the dead, and your members as instruments of righteousness unto God. (Romans 6:13)*

So what is the Christian calling, on the basis of all this? It is a calling, moment by moment, to be dead to all things, that we might be alive to God at this moment.

We must notice, however, that this is not a sheer passivity. Often, it seems to me, Christians have missed the whole point here by relating this merely to some sort of passivity. But that would be simply a nonbiblical mysticism, not much more than the pagan Stoic concept of Marcus Aurelius. That would be merely a resignation, the French word *accepter*. It is like the beast in the field that cannot move. But it is not this way in the Scriptures. I am still a man, made in the image of God. "Yield ye your members," commands Paul—*yield* (Romans 6:13). It is not a state of passivity. You cannot bring forth the fruit, as we shall see later, but nevertheless you are not a figure of stone. God deals with you in the circle in which he made you, man in his own image.

"Know ye not, that to whom ye yield yourselves servants to obey [but you do the yielding], *his servants ye are whom ye obey; whether of sin unto death, or of obedience unto righteousness? But God be thanked, that ye were the servants of sin, but ye have obeyed from the heart that form of doctrine* [teaching; there is a content involved here, not a mere existential experience] *which was*

delivered you. Being then made free from sin, ye became the servants of righteousness. I speak after the manner of men because of the infirmity of your flesh: for as ye have yielded your members servants to uncleanness and to iniquity unto iniquity; even so now yield your members servants to righteousness unto holiness. (Romans 6:16-19)

Feel the force of the "activeness" in the midst of the passivity. "Yield yourselves": every man must be a creature. He can be nothing else but a creature in this life or in the life to come. Even in hell, men will still be creatures, because that is what we are. Only one is self-sufficient in himself, and he is God. But now as Christians we are introduced to the great reality: our calling is to be creatures in this high, tremendous, and glorious way, not because we must be, but *by choice.*

Marcus Aurelius, the pagan, knew only a resignation. That is no more than being a creature because you must be a creature. Carl Gustav Jung knew a giving-in, a mere submission to the things that roll over us from the collective unconsciousness of our race, or from that which is without. But this is mere resignation, whereas the scriptural teaching is *not* mere resignation. I am a creature, it is true, but I have a calling to be the creature *glorified.* I must be the creature, but I do not have to be the creature like the clod in the field, the cabbage that is rotting in the field as the snows melt. I am called to be a creature by choice, on the basis of Christ's finished work, by faith: the creature glorified.

Now I am ready for the war. Now there can be spirituality of a biblical sort. Now there can be a Christian life. Rejected, slain, raised: now we are ready to be used. But not only ready to be used in this present space-time world, but ready to enjoy it as the creature, ready to enjoy it in the light of its createdness by God and my own finiteness, and ready to enjoy it, yet seeing it as it is since the Fall. Justification is once for all. At one moment my guilt is declared gone forever, but this is not once for all. This is a moment-by-moment thing—a moment-by-moment being dead to all else and alive to God, a moment- by-moment stepping back by faith into the present world as though we had been raised from the dead. Here is the real positive, after the proper negative.

CHAPTER 4

IN THE SPIRIT'S POWER

In this chapter we turn our attention again to the Mount of Transfiguration and think not only of Christ's resurrection, but also of the Christian's resurrection. Of course, the liberal theologians would tell us that the notion of a physical resurrection is a late idea, but I don't think this will stand at all. The physical resurrection appears very early in God's revelation of hope to man.

> *So man lieth down, and riseth not: till* [there is a very definite note of the until-ness here] *the heavens be no more, they shall not awake, nor be raised out of their sleep. O that thou wouldest hide me in the grave* [sheol, and it is definitely sheol], *that thou wouldest keep me secret, until* [here we come to that intriguing word until again] *thy wrath be past, that thou wouldest appoint me a set time, and remember me! If a man die, shall he live again? all the days of my appointed time will I wait, till* [this intriguing word again] *my change come. (Job 14:12-14, emphasis added)*

The thrust here is all *until:* until my release comes.

It seems to me that Job 14 is absolute, that Job, somewhere around 2000 B.C. or earlier, understood the reality of a physical resurrection. I think the nineteenth chapter teaches the same thing, but in the Hebrew it is not as clear as it is in chapter 14.

In Hebrews 11:17-19 it says that Abraham (at 2000 B.C.) understood the truth of the resurrection: "By faith Abraham, when he was tried, offered up Isaac: and he that had received the promises offered up his only begotten son. Of whom it was said, That in Isaac shall thy seed be called: accounting that God was able to raise him up, even from the dead."

So Abraham, who lived in the same general time as Job, did understand the fact of resurrection. Therefore, it is not surprising to find it in the book of Job. So there is no reason to think, as the liberals would have us

41

think, that every time we find an emphasis on resurrection, it must be put late in biblical history.

In Daniel, which of course is not anywhere near so early, there is also an emphasis on physical resurrection not of Christ, but of man: "And many of them that sleep in the dust of the earth shall awake, some to everlasting life, and some to shame and everlasting contempt" (Daniel 12:2). There is here an emphasis of double resurrection, the lost as well as the saved: "They that be wise shall shine as the brightness of the firmament; and they that turn many to righteousness as the stars for ever and ever" (12:3). These things are surely related. But the most exciting, I guess, is verse 13, where Daniel himself is told by God, "But go thy way till the end be: for thou shalt rest, and stand in thy lot at the end of the days." What we are told here is that at the end of the days, *Daniel himself* will share in the events which he has just seen in prophecy. So the physical resurrection of the believer is clearly taught in Scripture early in biblical history.

When we come to 1 Corinthians 15, in the New Testament, there is no debate that this is exactly what Paul is teaching. He is hanging everything on this:

> *Now if Christ be preached that he rose from the dead, how say some among you that there is no resurrection of the dead? But if there is no resurrection of the dead, then is Christ not risen: and if Christ be not risen, then is our preaching vain, and your faith is also vain. Yea, and we are found false witnesses of God; because we have testified of God that he raised up Christ: whom he raised not up, if so be that the dead rise not. (15:12-15)*

The argument is very simple. If the Christian dead are not raised up, then Christ was not raised up; and if Christ is not raised up, everything falls to the ground.

> *For if the dead rise not, then is not Christ raised: and if Christ be not raised, your faith is vain; ye are yet in your sins. Then they also which are fallen asleep in Christ are perished. If in this life only we have hope in Christ, we are of all men most miserable. But now is Christ risen from the dead, and become the firstfruits of them that slept. For since by man came death, by man came also the resurrection of the dead. For as in Adam all die, even so in Christ shall all be*

made alive. But every man in his own order: Christ the firstfruits; afterward they that are Christ's at his coming. Then cometh the end, when he shall have delivered up the kingdom to God, even the Father; when he shall have put down all rule and all authority and power. For he must reign, till he hath put all enemies under his feet. The last enemy that shall be destroyed is death." (15:16-26)

Now as we turn to the Mount of Transfiguration, it would seem to me that we have a clear preview of this. One would not wish to be dogmatic, but it would seem that we have represented—or at least illustrated, depending on how strongly one feels about it—that which will happen on Resurrection Day. We have here Moses, who represents the Old Testament dead, and we have the apostles, who represent the New Testament dead. But we also have Elijah, who, of course, is one of the two men of the Old Testament who are spoken of as "the translated ones." And the Pauline Epistles make it very plain that at the coming of Jesus Christ for his people, there will be translated ones.

Behold, I show you a mystery; we shall not all sleep, but we shall all be changed, in a moment, in the twinkling of an eye, at the last trump: for the trumpet shall sound, and the dead shall be raised incorruptible, and we shall be changed. For this corruptible must put on incorruption, and this mortal must put on immortality. So when this corruptible shall have put on incorruption, and this mortal shall have put on immortality, then shall be brought to pass the saying that is written, Death is swallowed up in victory. O death, where is thy sting? O grave, where is thy victory? The sting of death is sin; and the strength of sin is the law. But thanks be to God, which giveth us the victory through our Lord Jesus Christ. Therefore, my beloved brethren, be ye stedfast, unmoveable, always abounding in the work of the Lord, forasmuch as ye know that your labour is not in vain in the Lord. (1 Corinthians 15:51-58)

So here we have translation as well as resurrection. This is a historic situation; it is not in the never-never land of mere religious psychology or religious philosophy. At some moment—and there will be believers on the earth until the last moment—Christ will come and the dead will be raised. But the Christians who will be living then will be changed in the twinkling of an eye, in space and in time. Interestingly, verse 58 sets the resurrection and then the translation together in relation to our present life, calling for a response in the present situation. On the basis of these things, be *in the present life* steadfast, and so on.

In the First Epistle to the Thessalonians we have exactly the same thing: the same note of translation as well as resurrection.

> *But I would not have you to be ignorant, brethren, concerning them which are asleep, that ye sorrow not, even as others which have no hope. For if we believe that Jesus died and rose again, even so them also which sleep in Jesus will God bring with him. For this we say unto you by the word of the Lord, that we which are alive and remain unto the coming of the Lord shall not prevent them which are asleep. For the Lord himself shall descend from heaven with a shout, with the voice of the archangel, and with the trump of God: and the dead in Christ shall rise first: then we* [the Christians of that time] *which are alive* [in that historic moment] *and remain shall be caught up together with them in the clouds, to meet the Lord in the air: and so shall we ever be with the Lord. (1 Thessalonians 4:13-17)*

And then, interestingly enough, Paul makes this a reason for a call at this present moment: "Wherefore comfort one another with these words" (4:18).

However, this brings us to another question: It is very fine that I am going to be raised from the dead, but what happens between the Christian's death and his resurrection? Am I going to be out of contact with history? Am I going to be out of contact with sequence? Is the Christian, between his death and his resurrection, *nowhere*? Does he just disappear into a void?

The answer is no, and the Scripture is very plain. In Luke 23:43, for example, where Jesus is speaking to the dying thief on the cross, he promises him that "today [that day, in that area of sequence, before sundown, because this would be the end of the Jewish day] "shalt thou be with me in paradise." Instead of being nowhere, in a philosophic "other," he will be with Christ in paradise.

Paul says the same thing, it seems to me, with great finality, in 2 Corinthians 5:4-8:

For we that are in this tabernacle [that is, we who are in this body, who are alive] *do groan, being burdened: not for that we would be unclothed, but clothed upon, that mortality might be swallowed up of life. Now he that hath wrought us for the selfsame thing is God, who also hath given unto us the earnest of the Spirit. Therefore we are always confident, knowing that, whilst we are at home in the body, we are absent from the Lord: (For we walk by faith, not by sight:) We are confident, I say, and willing rather to be absent from the body, and to be present with the Lord.*

The Bible presents only two states for the Christian: to be here in the flesh or, having died, to be with the Lord. It is exactly the same thing as Jesus presents on the cross. The Christian is not presented, at the time of death, as being out of contact with sequence, as being nowhere, any more than Jesus is out of contact with sequence or is nowhere between his resurrection and his second coming.

There are a great number of dead who crowd into our thinking, of course, at this point. This is not just a theological question; it is a very practical one. We think of the masses of the Old Testament believing dead and the masses of the New Testament believing dead. We think of our loved ones who are involved in this. Where are they? And we have ourselves, too, to think about. We may die before Jesus comes back, though each of us should have the hope that he will be here when Jesus comes back. And if we die, where will we be an hour after death and until Jesus comes?

The world's view, of course, immediately places the afterlife as either a nothing or as being in a shrouded area: a place of sheets and formlessness, something that comes in under the door or through the keyhole as a gray mist. The new liberal theology would take the afterlife and either deny it or make it such an uncertain quality that it has no meaning to us. But this is not true of the Bible. Standing on the Mount of Transfiguration, we see Elijah, who was translated yet has a body. There is no reason to think it is otherwise. He is holding a conversation with Moses and Christ. But here is Moses as well—Moses who died and was buried. And yet he can share in the conversation and he can be seen. He can be recognized and there can be communication.

We have the same sort of situation with Samuel and Saul. There is no reason to think of this as being anything other than Samuel's spirit, and yet there is communication, there is recognition.

But even stronger than that is Jesus' own word when he had been raised from the dead. When Jesus was raised from the dead, the disciples thought he was a spirit. They were not naturalists, but supernaturalists. They would not really have been surprised at having seen a spirit. What they were not prepared for was the physical resurrection. So Jesus says to them—very sharply, really—in love, but sharply: "A spirit hath not flesh and bones, as ye see me have" (Luke 24:39). And then, in contrast, the statement that follows this in Luke is "Give me something to eat." His saying was, Give me something to eat, and I will show you that I am not just a spirit. It was not, How can you be so stupid as to think you could see me if I were a spirit? How could you be so stupid as to think that you could converse with me if I were a spirit? He did not say this. He immediately opened the door to the fact that it was not to be regarded as surprising that they could see him. They were not stupid in thinking they could converse with him if he was only a spirit. The proof was not in seeing him, nor in conversation with him. The proof concerning the physical resurrection was the eating of food before them.

So Moses, who was dead, stood on the mountain. And we are faced with a continuing stream of redeemed, conscious individuals who have died. We have no reason to feel they are anything but recognizable. We have no reason to think of them as lonely spirits, shut off from communication with Christ, with each other. The call to the Christian, as he looks forward to possible death, is not to be afraid, but to realize that, at the moment of death, if he has accepted Christ as Savior, he can pass into that moment, "today," *whatever our today is*. We do not need to be afraid to die. No doubt the central thing given is that the Christian dead are with Christ. There is no reason to think that they are out of communication with Christ as soon as they die. To be absent from the body is to be present with the Lord—not merely conscious, but with the Lord.

Now, however, I would want to emphasize something more, in the sense of giving it additional force. From the scriptural viewpoint this is not given just as a psychological hope. The dead are really there in this conscious and real state with Christ. They are there. This is a part of the total universe. It is as much a part of the total universe as you are as you are sitting reading this. Not in a philosophic "other" again, but in reality, they are really there. Time is important. The thief was not there till he got there.

Sequence is meaningful. Sequence is meaningful to the thief on the cross, as time moves on to that glad moment when the clock strikes, and he comes back with Jesus Christ. Time moves on. To the thief on the cross, though he does not have his body yet, there is a sequence.

However, the point I would establish at this stage in our study of spirituality is the fact that there are two equal lines of reality presented to us in the universe. We are in the seen world and there are also the Christians who have died, who are with Christ now. It is not a primitive view, a kind of three-story concept of the universe. This is the biblical view of truth: there are two streams, two strands, a space-time reality—one in the seen, and one in the unseen.

With these two lines before us, two equal lines of reality, I would return to the conclusion of our previous chapter. When God tells us to live as though we had died, gone to heaven, seen the truth there, and come back to this world, he is not asking us merely to act on some psychological motivation, but on what really is. That is the second line, the second strand, of reality, that of the unseen, in which we personally will share between the moment of death and our return with resurrected bodies to the seen world at the Second Coming. Thus *I am to live now* by faith, rooted in the things which *have been*, such as Christ's death and resurrection; what *is*, such as the second stream of reality in the unseen now; and what *will be*, such as my coming bodily resurrection and return with Christ. And this is not sheer passivity, as we have seen. God will deal with me in the circle in which he made me; that is, in his image—as a man, not as a stick or a stone. There are *unbiblical* forms of "spirituality" that put their emphasis almost entirely upon some sort of resignation. The Bible rejects this. You are not just a beast in the field. It is not just a case of accepting, there is to be an *activeness* in our passivity. We have to be creatures because that is what we are—creatures. But in Christ we are presented with an opportunity, a calling, to be a creature by *choice*, to be creatures glorified. Through an active passivity, we are creatures, not of necessity but by choice, here in this present, space-time, historic world. When I come to this point, no matter how many times I preach or teach it, it still takes my breath away.

Yet to be practical I must ask, *How* is it possible to live so? What is the answer to the how? How are we going to live this way, if we are to think of this not merely as some sort of abstract "religious" experience, a combination of mood and moment, a vague, contentless, meaningless existential experience? If I am not to think of it in this way, I must face the question of the how. What do I begin to do? Do I begin to whip myself in order to get it accomplished? Do I begin to seek some sort of ecstasy or exotic experience?

The answer to all these is no. Happily, this is not given to us merely as some kind of twentieth-century religious idea. It is an intensely practical one.

For we that are in this tabernacle do groan [you recognize this as the passage we have already studied], *being burdened: not for that we would be unclothed, but clothed upon, that mortality might be swallowed up of life. Now he that hath wrought us for the selfsame thing is God, who also hath given unto us the earnest of the Spirit. (2 Corinthians 5:4, 5)*

In other words, God draws two factors of reality together here: the factor of our being with Christ when we die, and the factor that at the present time, with equal certainty, if we have accepted Christ as Savior, we are indwelt by the Holy Spirit. It is intriguing that God brings these two factors together. He does not expect us to think of them separately. When I die, it is certain that I will be with the Lord. The Christian dead, including my loved ones, are there with him now. But at the same time, at the present moment, I have the Holy Spirit.

And the same thing is presented, it seems to me, in Hebrews 12:22-24, where these two concepts are united: "But ye are come unto mount Sion [Who is come? Those who have accepted Christ as Savior and are still in this life], and unto the city of the living God, the heavenly Jerusalem, and to an innumerable company of angels, to the general assembly and church of the firstborn, which are written in heaven, and to God the Judge of all, and to the spirits of just men made perfect."

Here we are told that we are *now* united with these people, and this, of course, leads us to the doctrine of the mystical union of the church (those living now and those who have died) but I am not here thinking of it as a doctrine. I am thinking of the reality: that God ties us in at the present time to the reality of those who are already in this other situation. They are there, they see Christ face-to-face, they are dead, and we have the earnest of the Holy Spirit.

With this in mind let us think of Galatians 2:20, which we have already looked at several times in this study: "I am crucified with Christ: nevertheless I live; yet not I, but Christ liveth in me: and the life which I now live in the flesh [that is, before I have died] I live by faith in the Son of God, who loved me, and gave himself for me."

This verse falls into three different portions: "I am crucified with

Christ: [a break] "nevertheless I live; [a break] yet not I, but Christ liveth in me, and the life which I now live in the flesh I live by faith in the Son of God who loved me, and gave himself for me."

Here we are told that Christ really lives in me if I have accepted Christ as my Savior. In other words, we have the words of Jesus to the thief on the cross, "Today shalt thou be with me in paradise" (Luke 23:43). Christ can say, "Today shalt thou be with me in paradise" and mean it. To die is to be with the Lord. It is not just an idea; it is a reality. But at the same time, Christ, the same Christ, gives the promise just as definitely that when I have accepted Christ as my Savior, he lives in me. *They are equal reality.* They are two streams of present reality, both equally promised. The Christian dead are already with Christ now, and Christ really lives in the Christian. Christ lives in me. The Christ who was crucified—the Christ whose work is finished, the Christ who is glorified now—has promised (John 15) to bring forth fruit in the Christian, just as the sap of the vine brings forth the fruit in the branch.

Here is true Christian mysticism. Christian mysticism is not the same as non-Christian mysticism, but I would insist that it is not a lesser mysticism. Indeed, eventually it is a deeper mysticism, for it is not based merely on contentless experience, but on historic, space-time reality—on propositional truth. One is not asked to deny the reason, the intellect, in true Christian mysticism. And there is to be no loss of personality, no loss of the individual man. In Eastern mysticism—for which the West is searching so madly now that it has lost the sense of history, of content, and the truth of biblical facts—there is always finally a loss of the personality. It cannot be otherwise in their framework. You will remember the story of Shiva, who is one of the Hindu manifestations of the Everything. He came and loved a mortal woman. Shiva put his arms around the woman in his love, and immediately she disappeared, and he became neuter. This is Eastern mysticism. It is grounded in the loss of personality of the individual. Not so in Christian mysticism. Christian mysticism is communion with Christ. It is Christ bringing forth fruit through me, the Christian, with no loss of personality and without my being used as a stick or a stone, either.

In many passages in the Bible, the relationship of Christians to Jesus Christ is described in terms of the bride and the bridegroom. Who is this "bridegroom"—my bridegroom? He is the Christ who has died, whose work is finished, who is raised, who is ascended, who is glorified. It is this Christ. It is not simply an idea. It is the Christ who was seen after the Resurrection, the Christ who was seen by Stephen, by Paul, the Christ who was seen by John; it is *this* Christ who is my bridegroom. It can be properly said that in this sense we are all female. Christ is the bridegroom; we—that is, Christians—are the bride.

> *Likewise reckon ye also yourselves to be dead indeed unto sin, but alive unto God through Jesus Christ our Lord. (Romans 6:11)*

In this section dealing with sanctification, beginning with Romans 5, these words "through Christ" run throughout like the string on which all the beads are to be placed.

> *Therefore being justified* [in the past] *by faith we have peace with God* [in the present] *through our Lord Jesus Christ. (Romans 5:1)*

> *O wretched man that I am! who shall deliver me from the body of this death? I thank God through Jesus Christ our Lord. (Romans 7:24-25)*

> *Nay, in all these things we are more than conquerors through him that loved us. (Romans 8:37)*

Christ is with those in paradise now. But Christ—the same Christ, with the same reality—promises the Christian that he will bring forth fruit through us in this life now. The power of the crucified, risen, and glorified Christ will bring forth this fruit through us now.

Now, as we come to the end of our study of the basic considerations of the Christian life and the true spirituality, and before we proceed into further considerations, let us finish with three points in mind.

First, the answers of the how: It is not to be done simply in our own strength. Neither is it only acting in practice upon the reality that in God's sight, as we are in Christ, judicially we are already dead and raised, as wonderful as that is. That must never be minimized. It is a real thing that must be comprehended. Judicially, this is a reality, because Christ has died, and Christ has paid. We are not trying to make something that does not have a reality. But it is more than just acting upon this fact, even though it is so wonderful and should fill us with adoration. It is much more. The how is that the glorified Christ will do it through us. There is an active ingredient: He will be the doer.

Second, though we will enlarge on this point later, there is the agency of the Holy Spirit: "And hope maketh not ashamed; because the love of God has been shed abroad in our hearts by the Holy Ghost [Spirit] which is given unto us" (Romans 5:5).

What he is saying here is that you will not be ashamed experientially when you begin to act upon the reality, upon the teaching, as it has been presented. Why? "Because the love of God is shed abroad in our hearts by the Holy Spirit which is given to us."

Paul writes further, "But now we are delivered from the law, that being dead wherein we were held; that we should serve in newness of spirit, and not in the oldness of the letter" (Romans 7:6).

What makes the difference? This is the Holy Spirit, not just a "new idea." *It is not to be in our own strength.* There is a Holy Spirit who has been given to us to make this service possible.

In Romans 1–8, at the end of the section on the development of the Christian's sanctification, the work of the Holy Spirit, the agent of the whole Trinity, is brought into full force in the eighth chapter.

In Romans 8:13 this is drawn together in this great central chapter of the work of the Holy Spirit *for* and *to* the Christian: "For [because] if you live after the flesh, ye shall die; but if ye through the Spirit do mortify the deeds of the body, ye shall live." The Holy Spirit is specifically introduced to us here as the agent of the power and the person of the glorified Christ. There is not enough strength in ourselves, but placed before us is the power and the work of the glorified Christ through the agency of the Holy Spirit. Surely this is exactly what Christ meant when he said: 'I will not leave you comfortless [as orphans]. I will come to you" (John 14:18).

Though we cannot develop it at length, 2 Corinthians 13:14, which we usually use as a benediction, makes the same point: "The grace of the Lord Jesus Christ, and the love of God [the Father], and the communion of the Holy Spirit, be with you all." The communion, or the communication, of the Holy Spirit speaks of the Holy Spirit as the agent of the Trinity, wherein Christ could promise in John 14 not only that Christ would not leave us as orphans, but that both he and the Father would come to us. Surely, as we look at the book of Acts, we find in the early church not a group of strong men laboring together, but the work of the Holy Spirit bringing to them the power of the crucified and glorified Christ. It must be so for us also.

Third, this is not to be merely passive on our part. As we have seen already, it is not to be on the basis of our own works, or our own energy, any more than our justification is on the basis of our own works and energy. But again, as in the case of justification, I am not a passive stick or stone.

The illustration which brings this to me with force is Mary's response to the angel (Luke 1:38). The angel has come to Mary, and says, in effect, Mary, you are going to give birth to the long-promised Messiah. This was a unique promise, and unrepeatable. There is something totally unique here: the birth of the eternal second Person of the Trinity into this world. What is her response? The Holy Spirit, we are told, is to cause a conception in her womb. It seems to me that she could have made three responses. She was a Jewish girl, probably seventeen or eighteen years of age, and in love with Joseph. There is no reason to think of him as an old man, as the painters love to paint, no reason whatsoever. They do that because this was a Roman Catholic mentality, as though Joseph and Mary had no children of which they were both the parents, after Christ's birth.

Here she is, a Jewish girl, seventeen or eighteen years old, in love with Joseph, in a normal historic situation, with normal emotions, and suddenly she is told she is going to give birth to a child. She could have rejected the idea and said, "I do not want it. I want to withdraw; I want to run. What would Joseph say?" And we know what Joseph thought later. Humanly, we could not blame her if she had felt this way. But she did not say this.

Second—and this is our danger at such a point as we now are in the study of the Christian life—she could have said, "I now have the promises, so I will exert my force, my character, and my energy, to bring forth the promised thing. I have the promise. Now I will bring forth a child without a man." But with this response she never would have had the child. She could not bring forth a child without a man, by her own will, any more than any other girl could do.

But there was a third thing she could say. It is beautiful; it is wonderful. She says, "Behold, the handmaid of the Lord; be it unto me according to thy word."

There is an active passivity here. She took her own body, by choice, and put it into the hands of God to do the thing that he said he would do, and Jesus was born. She gave herself, with her body, to God. In response to the promise, yes; but not to do it herself. This is a beautiful, exciting, personal expression of a relationship between a finite person and the God she loves. Now this is absolutely unique and must not be confused; there is only one Virgin Birth. Nevertheless, it is an illustration of our being the bride of Christ. We are in the same situation in that we have these great and thrilling promises we have been considering, and we are neither to think of ourselves as totally passive, as though we had no part in this, as though God had stopped dealing with us now as men; nor are we to think we can do it ourselves. If we are to bring forth fruit in the Christian life, or rather, if Christ is to bring forth this fruit through us by the agency of the Holy Spirit, there must be a constant act of faith, of thinking, *Upon the basis of your promises I am looking for you to fulfill them, O my Jesus Christ; bring forth your fruit through me into this poor world.*

That is what I mean by active passivity, and it is no longer a dead word, I trust; it is beautiful. There should be the sound of trumpets and the clanging of cymbals; there should be the psalm upon the many-stringed instruments. We are not irrevocably caught. We do not have to beat ourselves, or be dejected. "Be it unto me according to thy word."

So now we stand before two streams of reality: those who have died and are with Christ now; and we, who have the "earnest" of the Holy Spirit now and so, upon the reality of the finished work of Christ, have access—not in theory, but in reality—to the power of the crucified, risen, and glorified Christ, by the agency of the Holy Spirit.

True spirituality is not achieved in our own energy. The "how" of the kind of life we have spoken of, the true Christian life, true spirituality, is Romans 6:11: "Reckon ye also yourselves [there is the faith; then the negative aspect] to be dead indeed unto sin, [but then the positive] but alive unto God through Jesus Christ our Lord." This is the "how," and there is no other. It is the power of the crucified, risen, and glorified Christ, through the agency of the Holy Spirit by faith.

CHAPTER 5

THE SUPERNATURAL UNIVERSE

Our generation is overwhelmingly naturalistic. There is an almost complete commitment to the concept of the uniformity of natural causes in a closed system. This is its distinguishing mark. If we are not careful, even though we say we are biblical Christians and supernaturalists, nevertheless the naturalism of our generation tends to come in upon us. It may infiltrate our thinking without our recognizing its coming, like a fog creeping in through a window opened only half an inch. As soon as this happens, Christians begin to lose the reality of their Christian lives. As I travel about and speak in many countries, I am impressed with the number of times I am asked by Christians about the loss of reality in their Christian lives. Surely this is one of the greatest, and perhaps the greatest reason for a loss of reality: that while we say we believe one thing, we allow the spirit of the naturalism of the age to creep into our thinking unrecognized. All too often the reality is lost because the "ceiling" is down too close upon our heads. It is too low. And the ceiling which closes us in is the naturalistic type of thinking.

Now the Christian's spirituality, as we wrote of it in the previous chapters, does not stand alone. It is related to the unity of the Bible's view of the universe. This means that we must understand—intellectually, with the windows open—that the universe is not what our generation says it is, seeing only the naturalistic universe. This relates directly to what we have been dealing with in the earlier chapters. For example, we have said that we are to love God enough to say "Thank you," even for the difficult things. We must immediately understand, as we say this, that this has no meaning whatsoever unless we live in a personal universe in which there is a personal God who objectively exists.

Later, we touched upon the same thing when we saw that, in the normal perspective, it is very difficult to say no to things and to self, in the things-mentality and the self-mentality of men, especially in the twentieth century. But we saw that on the Mount of Transfiguration we are brought face-to-face with a supernatural universe. Here we find Moses and Elijah speaking to Christ as he is glorified. And we observed that this supernatural universe is not a far-off universe. Quite the contrary: there is a perfect continuity, as in normal life. So (in Luke 9:37) the day after these things had occurred, Jesus and the disciples went down the mountain and entered into the normal activities of life. Indeed, the normal sequence was continuing while they were there on the mountain. There is a perfect example of the temporal and spatial relationship here. As they climbed up the mountain, there was no place where they passed into the philosophic "other." And if they had had watches upon their wrists, these watches would not have stopped at some point; they would have ticked away. And when they came down, it was the next day and the normal sequence had proceeded. Here we find the supernatural world in relationship to the normal sequence and spatial relationships of this present world.

We have also considered Christ's redemptive death, which has no meaning whatsoever outside the relationship of a supernatural world. The only reason the words "redemptive death" have any meaning is that there is a personal God who exists and, more than that, has a character. He is not morally neutral. When man sins against this character, which is the law of the universe, he is guilty, and God will judge that man on the basis of true moral guilt. In such a setting, the words "the redemptive death of Christ" have meaning, otherwise they cannot.

Now we must remember what we are talking about: the fact that the true Christian life, as we have examined it, is not to be separated from the unity of the full biblical teaching; it is not to be abstracted from the unity of the Bible's emphasis on the supernatural world. This makes sense of the biblical image of Christians, face-to-face with this supernatural world, as the bride, linking themselves to Christ, the bridegroom, so that he, the crucified, risen, and glorified Christ, may bring forth fruit through them. This is no longer a surprising doctrine.

Yet I have a feeling that even people who have been well taught about salvation, and many other aspects of Christian life or doctrine, often find the idea of Christ the bridegroom bringing forth fruit through Christians as his bride a rather exotic and surprising or at least, abstract, doctrine. But surely this cannot be a surprising doctrine, if it is not isolated from the teaching of the Bible concerning the supernaturalness of the total universe in which we live.

This is the Bible's message, and when we see it so, and are in this framework, rather than the naturalistic one (which comes in so easily upon us), the teaching that Christ is the bridegroom will bring forth fruit through me ceases to be strange. The Bible insists that we live in reality in a supernatural universe. But if we remove the objective reality of the supernatural universe in any area, this great reality of Christ the bridegroom bringing forth fruit through us immediately falls to the floor, and all that Christianity is at such a point is a psychological and sociological aid, a mere tool. As soon as we remove the supernaturalness of the universe, all we have left is Aldous Huxley's *Brave New World,* in which religion is to be simply a sociological tool for the future. In Julian Huxley's concept of romantic evolutionary humanism, religion has a place, not because there is any truth in it, but because in the strange evolutionary formation, man as he now is simply needs it. So it must be administered to him, because he needs it. Remove the supernatural from the universe, in thinking and in action, and there is nothing left but *Honest to God,* which deals only with the fact of anthropology, and has nothing to say to questions of the reality of communication with God. We are merely shut up to anthropology, psychology, and sociology, and all that we say about religion in general—and Christianity specifically—falls to the ground except as it relates to a mere psychological mechanism. All the reality of Christianity rests upon the reality of the existence of a personal God, and the reality of the supernatural view of the total universe.

However, now I wish to move on to another positive concept, consequent to this. The true Bible-believing Christian is the one who lives *in practice* in this supernatural world. I am not saying that no one can be saved and go to heaven unless he lives in practice in this supernatural world. Happily, this is not so, or none of us would go to heaven, because none of us lives this way consistently. What I am saying is that the true Bible-believing Christian is one who does so. I am not a Bible-believing Christian in the fullest sense simply by believing the right doctrines, but as I live in practice in this supernatural world.

What does this mean? According to the biblical view, there are two parts to reality: the natural world—that which we see normally—and the supernatural part. When we use the word "supernatural," however, we must be careful. The supernatural is really no more unusual in the universe, from the biblical viewpoint, than what we normally call the natural. The only reason we call it the supernatural part is that usually we cannot see it. That is all. From the biblical view—the Judeo-Christian view—reality has two halves, like two halves of an orange. You do not have the whole orange unless you have both parts. One part is normally seen, and the other is normally unseen.

I would suggest that this may be illustrated by two chairs.[1] The men who sit in these chairs look at the universe in two different ways. We are all sitting in one or the other of these chairs at every single moment of our lives. The first man sits in his chair and faces this total reality of the universe, the seen part and the normally unseen part, and consistently sees truth against this background. The Christian is a man who has said, "I sit in this chair." The unbeliever, however, is the man who sits in the other chair, intellectually. He sees only the natural part of the universe, and interprets truth against that background. Let us see that these two positions cannot both be true. One is true: one is false. If indeed there is only the natural portion of the universe, with a uniformity of natural causes in a closed system, then to sit in the other chair is to delude oneself. If, however, there *are* the two halves of reality, then to sit in the naturalist's chair is to be extremely naïve and to misunderstand the universe completely. From the Christian viewpoint, no man has ever been so naïve, nor so ignorant of the universe, as twentieth-century man.

However, to be a true, Bible-believing Christian, we must understand that it is not enough simply to acknowledge that the universe has these two halves. The Christian life means living in the *two halves* of reality: the supernatural and the natural parts. I would suggest that it is perfectly possible for a Christian to be so infiltrated by twentieth-century thinking that he lives most of his life as though the supernatural were not there. Indeed, I would suggest that all of us do this to some extent. The supernatural does not touch the Christian only at the new birth and then at his death, or at the second coming of Christ, leaving the believer on his own in a naturalistic world during all the time in between. Nothing could be further from the biblical view. Being a biblical Christian means living in the supernatural now—not only theoretically, but in practice. If a man sits in the one chair and denies the existence of the supernatural portion of the world, we say he is an unbeliever. What shall we call ourselves when we sit in the other chair but live as though the supernatural were not there? Should not such an attitude be given the name "unfaith"? "Unfaith" is the Christian not living in the light of the supernatural now. It is Christianity that has become a dialectic, or simply a "good philosophy." As a matter of fact, I think very strongly that

---

[1] For a more complete treatment of this, see the last chapter of my book *Death in the City,* published by InterVarsity Press.

Christianity *is* a good philosophy. I think it is the best philosophy that ever has existed. More than this, it is the *only* philosophy that is consistent to itself and answers the questions. It is a good philosophy precisely because it deals with the problems and gives us answers to them. Nevertheless, it is not *only* a good philosophy. The Bible does not just speak in abstractions; it does not tell about a religious idea far away. It tells about man as Man. It tells about each individual, as each man is that individual. And it tells us how to live in the real universe as it is now. Remove this factor, and it becomes only a dialectic.

As I have said, I am in one chair or the other at any given moment. Unhappily, the Christian all too often tends to vacillate between the two chairs. At one moment he is in the chair of faith, and at another moment he is in the chair of unfaith. Once I have accepted Jesus Christ as Savior, I am saved because I rest in the hands of Jesus Christ and on the basis of his completely finished work. But God still deals with me as a man; I am not a machine, and I am not a figure of metal. It is perfectly possible for a Christian to alternate from one chair to another. But if I am trying to live a Christian life while sitting in the chair of unfaith, certain things are true. First of all, it is done in the flesh. I do not care what my activity may be; I do not care how much noise I make about soul-winning evangelism, or exotic things, for example. It is still in the flesh. I have put myself, the creature, at the center of the universe.

Second, if I am trying to live a Christian life while sitting in the chair of unfaith, I am only playing at it, rather than being in it, because the real battle is not against flesh and blood, but is in "high places," in the heavenlies (Ephesians 6:12). and I cannot participate in that battle in the flesh. In times of war, while the big brothers are away in the real battle, the little boys at home play soldiers. They act like soldiers all right, but they have no contact with nor any influence on the real battle being fought. When I try to live a Christian life while sitting in the chair of unfaith, I am just playing at war. I am not in contact with the real battle at all.

Third, the Lord will not honor our weapons if we are sitting in the chair of unfaith, because they do not give him any honor or glory. In fact, they steal the honor and glory from him, even that of being totally the Creator and the center of the universe. Paul speaks of this when he says, "Whatsoever is not of faith is sin" (Romans 14:23). Hudson Taylor said, "The Lord's work done in the Lord's way will never fail to have the Lord's provision." He was thinking primarily of material provision, but surely he would also include the whole provision. I would paraphrase his saying like this: "The Lord's work done in human energy is not the Lord's work any longer." It is something, but it is not the Lord's work.

At this point, two questions arise. The first is this: If the real battle is in the heavenlies, then are the heavenlies a long way off? And second, does not our individual part in it really become rather unimportant?

First, then, are the heavenlies, according to the Scriptures, a long way off? Is the supernatural world remote? The answer is, very decidedly, no. The Mount of Transfiguration makes it very, very plain that the supernatural world is not a long way off. One does not have to take a spaceship and fly for two generations, producing the second generation in flight, in order to reach the supernatural world. The supernatural in this case was at the top of the inclined plane of the mountain. There was sequence involved, so that when they came down, it was just the next step. This is the emphasis of Scripture, that the supernatural world is not far off, but very, very close indeed.

Speaking of Christ on the Emmaus road, Luke wrote: "And their eyes were opened, and they knew him; and he vanished out of their sight" (Luke 24:31).

It would in fact be better to translate: "He ceased to be seen of them." Luke does not say that Christ was no longer there. In this particular place they simply *did not see him* any longer. John 20:19 and 26 give the same emphasis. This view is not shut up to the one historic moment following the resurrection of Jesus Christ. It is the structure of the Scripture. The supernatural structure of the Scripture carries with it the emphasis that the supernatural is not far away but near at hand, all about us; the supernatural is not just yesterday and tomorrow, it is today.

This is equally to be found in the Old Testament: "And Jacob went on his way, and the angels of God met him. And when Jacob saw them he said, This is God's host: and he called the name of that place Mahanaim" (Genesis 32:1-2).

The Hebrew name "Mahanaim" means "two hosts" or "two camps." And one camp is as real as the other. One is not a shadow and fiction, a product of Jacob's mind. They were two equal hosts; in the first place, his own made up of his own family, and his animals, and all the rest; and the second one, angels, who were just as valid and real, and just as near at hand.

But perhaps the classic passage on this subject is 2 Kings 6:16-17. Here Elisha is surrounded by an enemy, and the young man who is with him is terrified. But Elisha says to him: "Fear not, for they that be with us are more than they that be with them." To the young man this must have seemed pretty cold comfort at that moment. But very quickly it became a realistic comfort, an actuality: "And Elisha prayed, and said, Lord, I pray thee, open his eyes, that he may see. And the Lord opened the eyes of the young man; and he saw: and, behold, the mountain was full of horses and chariots of fire round about Elisha." At that moment the young man did not have any more problems! From our present point of consideration, however, the significant thing is that the prayer was not that something would come. It was already there. The only difference was that the young man's eyes had to be opened to see what Elisha already saw. The supernatural was not something far off, it was there. All the young man needed was to have his eyes opened to see it.

When one refers to the supernatural, immediately the naturalistic man is determined to get rid of it. He is determined to argue that it is not there. That is why liberal theology—which is naturalistic—tries to make a theology that will stand when there is nothing left but anthropology. This is really where the battle of truth is being fought throughout the world. But if we see this, then we have thrust upon us the necessity, the high calling and the duty, to live in the light of the existence of the two parts of the universe, the seen and the unseen parts, in the realization that the heavenlies are not far off. They are about us here.

Now for the second question. If the real battles are supernatural, in the heavenlies, is not our part in them rather unimportant? A comment of the apostle Paul relates to this: "For I think that God has set forth us the apostles last, as it were appointed to death: for we are made a spectacle unto the world, and to angels, and to men" (1 Corinthians 4:9).

Here Paul makes the most fantastic claim, if one views it from merely a naturalistic viewpoint or sitting in the chair that we have called unfaith. The word in the Greek which is translated as "spectacle" has nothing to do with our modern use of that word. It is the idea of theater; we are on a stage being observed. He says here that the supernatural universe is not far off, and that while the real battle is in the heavenlies, our part is not unimportant at all, because it is being observed by the unseen world. It is like a one-way mirror. We are under observation.

Actually, this teaching does not rest upon this single verse. For example, Paul mentions it to Timothy, who in the narrow sense is not an apostle at all: "I charge thee before God, and the Lord Jesus Christ, and the elect angels . . . " (1 Timothy 5:21).

Is Timothy all alone? Is there a time when Timothy is not observed? The answer is no. God observes, but there is something more: the angels observe, too. And this is not only true of Timothy, but of us all. This, of course, is the meaning of the book of Job. Job did not understand that he was being observed, but he was. More than that, he was playing a part in the battle of the heavenlies, even though he did not know it, when the series of disasters struck. He was not only being observed, but there was a cause and effect relationship from the seen to the unseen world. We know this in the teaching of Christ, too, because Christ tells us that when a sinner repents, the angels in heaven rejoice. This is cause and effect, in twentieth-century language, a cause and effect relationship. There is a cause upon the earth and in the unseen world there is an effect. The supernatural world is not a long way off, and our part is not unimportant, because we are observed, and, more than that, there is a cause-and-effect relationship with the real battle in the heavenlies, on the basis of our living the Christian life or not.

If we keep in mind 1 Corinthians 4:9, where we are told that we are "on the stage" before men and angels, we must also note what Paul says in 1 Corinthians 2:4, which is not unrelated to this: "And my speech and my preaching was not with enticing words of man's wisdom, but in demonstration of the Spirit and of power."

In demonstration before whom? In the light of Paul's remarks in chapter 4, it is surely not only a demonstration before the lost world, or before the church, but a demonstration before the angels, too.

This verse has been grossly misunderstood. Many would say that it teaches that there should only be a "simple" preaching of the gospel, and by the simple preaching of the gospel they may mean the simple refusal to consider the questions of our own generation, and a simple refusal to wrestle with them. They contrast the simple preaching of the gospel with the attempt to give honest intellectual answers when honest questions are asked. But nothing could be further from the meaning of these words. That is "simply" not what these words are saying. What Paul is saying here is that the preaching of the gospel to simple or more "complicated" men fails in both cases if it does not include a demonstration of the Christian life, if it does not include the work of the Holy Spirit. It is not a matter of giving the simplest gospel message one can imagine, and making a complete dichotomy between faith and intellectual life. Paul is saying that no matter what kind of people you are preaching to, and no matter what terminology you need, and no matter how long the words you have to use, and whether you are speaking to the peasant or the philosopher, in every case there must be demonstration of the power of the Spirit—of the resurrected, glorified Christ working through us.

Little by little, many Christians in this generation find the reality slipping away. The reality tends to get covered by the barnacles of naturalistic thought. Indeed, I suppose this is one of half a dozen questions that are most often presented to me by young people from Christian backgrounds: Where is the reality? Where has the reality gone? I have heard it spoken in an honest, open desperation by fine young Christians in many countries. As the ceiling of the naturalistic comes down upon us, as it invades by injection or by connotation, reality gradually slips away. But the fact that Christ as the bridegroom brings forth fruit through me as the bride, through the agency of the indwelling Holy Spirit by faith, opens the way for me as a Christian to begin to know in the present life the reality of the supernatural. This is where the Christian is to live. Doctrine is important, but it is not an end in itself. There is to be an experiential reality, moment by moment. And the glory of the experiential reality of the Christian, as opposed to the bare existential experience, or the religious experiences of the East, is that we can do it with all the intellectual doors and windows open. We do not need a dark room; we do not need to be under the influence of a hallucinatory drug; we do not need to be listening to a certain kind of music; we can know the reality of the supernatural here and now.

This experiential result, however, is not just an experience of bare supernaturalism, without content, without our being able to describe and communicate it. It is much more. It is a moment-by-moment, increasing, experiential relationship to Christ and to the whole Trinity. We are to be in a relationship with the whole Trinity. The doors are open now—the intellectual doors, and also the doors to reality.

So this is the "how." This is how to live a life of freedom from the bonds of sin: not perfection, for that is not promised to us in this life. But this is how to have freedom in the present life from the bonds of sin, and from the results of those bonds, as we shall see later. This is the way we may exhibit the reality of the supernatural to a generation which has lost its way. This is the Christian life, and this is true spirituality. *In the light of the unity of the Bible's teaching in regard to the supernatural nature of the universe,* the how is the power of the crucified and the risen Christ, through the agency of the indwelling Holy Spirit, by faith.

CHAPTER 6

SALVATION:
PAST–FUTURE–PRESENT

The Bible says that man fell at a specific point in history, and as man fell, both man and the world over which he had dominion became abnormal. It would seem, looking at subsequent history, that God's creation of rational, moral creatures was a failure.

But then Christ came, died, and rose—also in history—and the necessary victory was won. When Christ returns, the evidence of his victory will be completely obvious. Yet on the earth today there is neither universal peace for the individual nor for mankind. Indeed, the twentieth-century world is not basically very different from the Assyrian, the Babylonian, or the Roman world.

Does that mean that between the victory on the cross and the present day, and on to the second coming of the Lord Jesus Christ, God did not intend that there should be any evidence of the reality of the victory of the cross?

As we examine Scripture, we surely find that this is exactly what he did *not* mean. "But ye are a chosen generation, a royal priesthood, an holy nation, a peculiar people [that is, a people set apart for a purpose]; that ye should show forth the praises [or the virtues] of him who hath called you out of darkness into his marvellous light: which in time past were not a people, but are now the people of God" (1 Peter 2:9-10).

This passage says that in this present life, Christians are called for a purpose, called to show forth the praises of God. In other words, God did not mean that there should be no evidence of the reality of the victory of the cross between Jesus' ascension and his second coming. God has always intended that Christians should be the evidence, the demonstration, of Christ's victory on the cross.

The Christian's call is to believe right doctrine, true doctrine, the doctrine of the Scripture. But it is not just a matter of stating right doctrine, though that is so important. Neither is it merely to be that which can be explained by natural talent, or character, or energy. The Christian is not called to present merely another message in the same way as all the other messages are presented. We must understand that it is not only important *what* we do, but *how we do it.* In the first chapter of the book of Acts, between Christ's resurrection and ascension, he gives a command not just to preach the gospel, but to *wait for the Holy Spirit* and then to preach the gospel. Preaching the gospel without the Holy Spirit is to miss the entire point of the command of Jesus Christ for our era. In the area of "Christian activities" or "Christian service," how we are doing it is at least as important as what we are doing. Whatever is not an exhibition that God exists misses the whole purpose of the Christian's life now on the earth. According to the Bible, we are to be living a supernatural life now, in this present existence, in a way we shall never be able to do again through all eternity. We are called upon to live a supernatural life now, by faith. Eternity will be wonderful, but there is one thing heaven will not contain, and that is the call, the possibility, and the privilege of living a supernatural life here and now by faith before we see Jesus face-to-face.

This is the demonstration that God intends in the world until Christ returns, and it is the Christian who is to be the demonstration. Christians are called upon to be a demonstration at our point of history that the supernatural, the normally unseen world, does exist and, beyond that, that God exists. They are to do this individually and corporately, each generation of Christians to their own generation. So we are to be the demonstration to the second half of the twentieth century. Obviously, we cannot be a demonstration to the past; and it can only be partially through our writings and our works that we leave a demonstration to the future, though there should be an accumulative demonstration, rolling up like a snowball through the centuries. But primarily, every Christian is to be a demonstration at his own point of history and to his own generation.

Christians are to demonstrate God's character, which is a moral demonstration, but it is not only to be a demonstration of moral principles; it is a demonstration of his being, his existence. What a calling, and how overwhelming! Surely anyone who has been at all honest, and not just romantic or idealistic in a bad sense, must understand that any such demonstrations would be totally meaningless by his own effort, in his own strength. So again, the biblical teaching of Christ as Bridegroom, bringing forth his fruit through us—the power of the crucified and risen Christ and the agency of the Holy Spirit by faith—is seen to be no isolated teaching. It should not take us by surprise. It fits into *the unity of the Bible's teaching about the calling of the Christian in this present world.* This is the second of the biblical unities that we have considered. The first was *the unity of the Bible's teaching in regard to the supernatural nature of the universe.*

A third unity of the Bible's teaching is *the unity of what salvation is.* When I truly accept Christ as my Savior, the Bible says God declares me justified at once. God, as the Judge, judicially declares the guilt gone upon the basis of the substitutionary work of Christ. It is not that God overlooks the sin. He is holy, and because he is holy, all sin results in true guilt. But when I accept Christ as my Savior, my sin has been punished in Christ: in history, space, and time, upon the cross. And God declares me justified as far as guilt is concerned. It is as though I had never sinned. On the cross Jesus took all of our punishment, which means there is no punishment left for us to bear, either in this life, or hereafter. Because Christ is divine his death had infinite value—value enough, in substitutionary fashion, to cover all of the individual sin, and all the guilt of all those who will ever come to him.

Justification must be understood to be absolutely irrevocable, for Christ took the punishment of *all* our sin, not just our sin up to the moment when we accepted Christ as our Savior. Nothing is left to be charged to our account. Seeing it this way, which is the biblical way to see it, there are no degrees of justification. One cannot be more or less justified. In this sense one cannot be more or less Christian. One is a Christian, or not a Christian, on this basis. Just as one is born or not born, married in God's sight or not married, so one has accepted Christ as Savior, and thus is declared justified by God, or not. There is no halfway, no degrees. Guilt is totally gone from the Christian, and gone forever. Therefore, for the Christian, justification is *past.*

But we must not make a mistake here. Salvation, as the word is used in Scripture, is wider than justification. There is a past, a future, and just as really, a present. The infinite work of Christ upon the cross brings to the Christian more than justification. In the *future*, there is glorification. When Christ returns, there will be the resurrection of the body, and eternity. But there is also a *present* aspect of salvation. Sanctification is our present relationship to our Lord, the present tense.

In sanctification there are degrees. We have said that there are no degrees of justification, because the guilt is absolutely gone. But in the question of our relationship to our Lord in the present time, there are degrees. There are degrees between different Christians, and we must also acknowledge degrees in our personal lives at different times.

The Christian life is not an unbroken, inclined plane. Sometimes it is up, and sometimes—we must all acknowledge if we are not deluding ourselves—it is down. While it is not possible to be more or less justified, it is possible to be more or less sanctified. Justification deals with the guilt of sin; sanctification deals with the power of sin in the Christian's life, and there are degrees in this.

Salvation is not just justification and then a blank until death; God never meant it to be so. Salvation is a unity, a flowing stream, from justification through sanctification to glorification:

> *And we know that all things work together for good to them that love God, to them who are the called according to his purpose. For whom he did foreknow, he also did predestinate to be conformed to the image of his Son, that he might be the firstborn among many brethren. Moreover whom he did predestinate, them he also called: and whom he called, them he also justified: and whom he justified, them he also glorified. (Romans 8:28-30)*

It is made plain, in the tenses that are used, that salvation is to be seen as an unbroken stream.

There are other examples of the same truth:

> *Therefore being justified by faith* [in the past], *we have peace* [in the present] *with God through our Lord Jesus Christ: by whom also we have access* [in the present] *by faith into this grace wherein we stand, and rejoice in hope of the glory of God. And not only so, but we glory in tribulations also: knowing that tribulation worketh patience; and patience, experience; and experience, hope: and hope maketh not ashamed* [does not disappoint us]; *because the love of God has been shed abroad in our hearts by the Holy Ghost which was given unto us. (Romans 5:1-5)*

Or we may take the keynote verses of the first half of the book of Romans:

> *For I am not ashamed of the gospel of Christ: for it is the power of God unto salvation to every one that believeth; to the Jew first, and also to the Greek. For therein is the righteousness of God revealed from faith to faith: as it is written, The just shall live by faith. (Romans 1:16-17)*

Now the word "salvation" here is not justification. The word "salvation" encompasses the whole: justification, sanctification, glorification. "For therein is the righteousness of God revealed from faith to faith." This is not just the "once for all" faith at justification, but faith "from faith to faith." "As it is written, The just shall live by faith"—not just be justified by faith: the just shall *live* by faith.

In certain ways, sanctification is the most important consideration for the Christian now, because that is the point where we are. It is the present portion of salvation, and in this sense it is the most important consideration of the Christian now. Justification is once for all; sanctification is continuous, from our acceptance of Christ right up to our death. This study of the Christian life and "true spirituality" falls within the present portion of our salvation. That is, this whole study is, in reality, a study of the biblical teaching of sanctification.

Salvation is a unity. When I accepted Christ as my Savior, when my guilt was gone, I returned to the place for which I was originally made. Man has a purpose. In this second half of the twentieth century, one is constantly confronted with the question, "What is the purpose of man—if man has any purpose?" And to that question the twentieth century returns a great silence. But the Bible says that man has the purpose of loving God with all his heart, with all his soul, and with all his mind. And this "loving" is not meant to be vague or "religious," in the modern sense, but a genuine communication with God: the finite person, thinking and acting and feeling, being in relationship with the infinite—not a bare infinite, but an infinite who is a personal God, and therefore communication is possible. This is the purpose of man, though lost through the fall. And when I accept Christ as my Savior, the guilt that has separated me from God, and from the fulfillment of my purpose, is removed. I then stand in the place in which man was made to stand at his creation. Not just in some far-off day, in the millennial reign of Christ, nor in eternity, but *now* I am returned to the place for which I was made at the beginning. I am immediately in *a new and living relationship with each of the three persons of the Trinity.* First, God the Father becomes my father. Theologically, this is spoken of as adoption. "But as many as received him, to them gave he power [or the right] to become the sons of God, even to them that believe on his name" (John 1:12). When I receive Christ, on the basis of his finished work I become a child of God. Christ, the second person of the Trinity, is uniquely the eternal Son of God. But the Bible declares, and it should be a joy to us, that when I have accepted

Christ as my Savior, I immediately come into a new relationship with the Father, and I become his son, in the sense of the creature in the proper place for which he was made in the first place.

Second, when I accept Christ as my Savior, I immediately come into a new relationship with God the Son. In theology this is spoken of as our mystical union with Christ. In the book of Ephesians we are told over and over again that when we accept Christ as our Savior we are "in" Christ. In Romans 7:4, we are told that Christ is our Bridegroom and we are the bride. In John 15 we are told that Christ is the Vine and we are the branches. In all these relationships there is pictured or related the mystical union of Christ and the believer. And who is this Christ, with whom we enter into a relationship? Not the baby Jesus, nor Christ when he was on earth, nor Christ as he hung on the cross, but the risen, ascended, and glorified Christ.

Finally, the Bible says we also enter into a new relationship with the third person of the Trinity, the Holy Spirit. When we are justified, we are also and immediately indwelt by the Holy Spirit. In John 14:16-17, Christ is making a promise just prior to his death, which was fulfilled at Pentecost after his resurrection and ascension: "I will pray the Father, and he shall give you another Comforter, that he may abide with you for ever; even the Spirit of truth; whom the world cannot receive, because it seeth him not, neither knoweth him: but ye know him; for he dwelleth with you, and shall be in you." There was a then-present relationship, but there would also be a future one. John explains this when he says that the Holy Spirit was not yet given, for Christ was not yet glorified (John 7:39). In the book of Romans, it is again made very plain that now if we have accepted Christ as our Savior, we are in this new relationship with the Holy Spirit, and anyone who is not in a relationship with the Holy Spirit is not a Christian. "But ye are not in the flesh, but in the Spirit, if so be that the Spirit of God dwell in you. Now if any man have not the Spirit of Christ, he is none of his" (8:9). Paul, writing to all the Christians at Corinth, asks, "Know ye not that ye are the temple of God, and that the Spirit of God dwelleth in you?" (1 Corinthians 3:16). This was written down through the ages to every man who has accepted Christ as Savior. When I am justified, I am indwelt by the Holy Spirit, and have entered into this new relationship with the third person of the Trinity.

Furthermore, we read this promise of Christ: "I will pray the Father, and he shall give you another Comforter, that he may abide with you for ever; even the Spirit of truth; whom the world cannot receive, because it seeth him not, neither knoweth him: but ye know him; for he dwelleth with you, and shall be in you. I will not leave you comfortless [or orphans]: I will come to you" (John 14:16-18). We are not "orphaned"; Christ comes to us through the agency of the indwelling Holy Spirit. And, in verse 23, connected with this, Jesus says: "And *we* will come unto him, and make our abode with him" (emphasis added). In this context the thrust is that the Holy Spirit indwelling the individual Christian is not only the agent of Christ, but he is also the agent of the Father. Consequently, when I accept Christ as my Savior, my guilt is gone, I am indwelt by the Holy Spirit, and I am in communication with the Father and the Son, as well as the Holy Spirit—the entire Trinity. Thus now, in the present life, if I am justified, I am in a personal relationship with each of the members of the Trinity. God the Father is my Father; I am in union with the Son; and I am indwelt by the Holy Spirit. This is not just meant to be doctrinal; *it is what I have now.*

Let me stress it again: salvation is all one piece. All salvation—past, present, and future—has one *base.* That base is not our faith. If we are confused here, then we are confused completely. A man can never be justified on the basis of his own faith. Through all of salvation the only base is the finished work of Jesus Christ on the cross in history. Faith is the empty hand, the *instrument* by which we accept God's free gift. Faith is simply believing God. It is not a leap in the dark. It is ceasing to call God a liar, and believing him. Justification is only on the basis of the finished work of Christ. Faith is the instrument by which we accept that finished work. This is the how, but this "how" extends through all salvation.

Consider, for example, assurance. The Bible makes it plain that the man who is a Christian has a right to know that he is saved: it is one of the good gifts of God, to know truly that he is a Christian. This refers not only to the initial fact, after one has accepted Christ as Savior, but also applies in those great and crushing moments in our lives when the waves get so high that it seems, psychologically or spiritually, that we can never find our footing again. At such a moment, a Christian can have assurance. His salvation rests on the finished work of Christ, whether he accepts the peace he should have or not, and he can have assurance *to the extent to which he believes the promises of God* at that moment.

It is exactly the same with sanctification. The basis is the finished work of Christ; the instrument to lay hold of that which God means us to have at this moment is faith. As a child of God, sanctification from the time of justification on, in the present life, is moment-by-moment. Justification is once for all, at that moment when, by God's grace, I accept Christ as my Savior; but sanctification is moment-by-moment, a moment-by-moment life of faith. At this particular place the existentialist is right when he points out the moment-by-moment character of man's life.

"For this is the love of God, that we keep his commandments: and his commandments are not grievous" (1 John 5:3). Is that true? In ourselves, do we find that his commandments are not grievous? I would say that for many years I found them grievous. For many years as a pastor, preaching the gospel, I never preached on this verse for the simple reason that I did not understand it. I found the commandments of God grievous; I could hardly bear them. And then one day, as I was wrestling with this topic, I saw that all one had to do was to look at the immediate context: "For this is the love of God, that we keep his commandments: and his commandments are not grievous. For whatsoever is born of God overcometh the world" (5:3-4). Fortunately it does not stop there, or it would not tell us the how. "And this is the victory that overcometh the world, even our faith" (5:4). On the basis of the finished work of Christ, a moment-by-moment life of faith is "the victory." Not our victory, but Christ's victory, purchased for us on Calvary's cross, laid hold of moment by moment in faith.

Sanctification and assurance are comparable. A man may be saved and not know he is saved because he does not raise the empty hands of faith at this particular moment and believe God's promises. And a man may lack in sanctification all that God means him to have in the present life because even though Christ has purchased it for him upon the cross he fails to believe God at this place and raise the empty hands of faith moment by moment. Now let me repeat, to be absolutely clear about it, the basis is not your faith; it is the finished work of Christ. Faith is the instrument to receive this thing from God that Christ has purchased for us.

So this is the third unity, *the unity of what salvation is:* a single piece, and yet a flowing stream. I became a Christian once for all upon the basis of the finished work of Christ through faith; that is justification. The Christian life, sanctification, operates on the same basis, but moment-by-moment. There is the same base (Christ's work) and the same instrument (faith); the only difference is that one is once-for-all and the other is *moment-by-moment.* The whole unity of biblical teaching stands solid at this place. If we try to live the Christian life in our own strength we will have sorrow, but if we live in this way, we will not only serve the Lord, but in place of sorrow, he will be our song. That is the difference. The how of the Christian life is the power of the crucified and risen Lord, through the agency of the indwelling Holy Spirit, by faith, *moment by moment.*

"Now the God of hope fill you with all joy and peace in believing, that ye may abound in hope, through the power of the Holy Spirit" (Romans 15:13). This is our calling, through the agency of the Holy Spirit. We are not called to serve God just any way, but to know joy and peace *in believing.*

CHAPTER 7

THE FRUITFUL BRIDE

When we accept Christ as our Savior, we are immediately in a new relationship with God the Father. God the Father is immediately *our* Father. He is *Abba*—Daddy—to us. But, of course, if this is so, we should be experiencing in this life the Father's *fatherliness*. When I accept Christ as my Savior, I also come into a new relationship with God the Son. He is at once my vine, my bridegroom. Now this raises a question. If I, as a branch and as a bride, am not bringing forth the fruit one would expect from him, who is my vine and my bridegroom—what is wrong?

> *Wherefore, my brethren, ye also are become dead to the law by the body of Christ;* [in order] *that ye should be married to another, even to him who is raised from the dead,* [in order] *that we should bring forth fruit unto God. (Romans 7:4)*

Notice the double "in order that": first, that we "should be married" to Christ; second, that we "should bring forth fruit unto God." But with that must go the very sober warning:

> *Neither yield ye your members as instruments* [tools, weapons] *of unrighteousness unto sin: but yield yourselves unto God as those that are alive from the dead, and your members* [yourselves as a unit and in part] *as instruments of righteousness unto God. (Romans 6:13)*

As a Christian I can yield myself to one or the other, in order that I might be used by one or the other, as a weapon in the warfare that is being fought.

> *For sin shall not have dominion over you: for ye are not under the law, but under grace. What then? shall we sin, because we are not*

under the law, but under grace? God forbid. Know ye not, that to whom ye yield yourselves servants [slaves] *to obey, his servants ye are to whom ye obey; whether of sin unto death, or of obedience unto righteousness? But God be thanked, that ye were the servants of sin, but ye have obeyed from the heart that form of doctrine* [teaching] *which was delivered you. Being then made free from sin, ye became the servants of righteousness. I speak after the manner of men because of the infirmity of your flesh: for as ye have yielded your members servants to uncleanness and to iniquity unto iniquity; even so now yield your members servants to righteousness unto holiness. For when ye were the servants of sin, ye were free from righteousness. What fruit had ye then* [before you were a Christian] *in those things whereof ye are now ashamed? for the end of those things is death. (Romans 6:14-21)*

This passage points out our high calling, to put ourselves by choice in the arms of our rightful lover, our bridegroom, in order to bring forth his fruit in the external world. But it also warns us that it is possible, even after we are Christians, to put ourselves into the arms of someone else and bring forth his fruit in this world. It is possible as a Christian to be bringing forth the same kind of fruit now as we did before we were Christians. Why? Because we are yielding ourselves to the wrong one, specifically to that old master of ours, the devil, Satan. Let us repeat it, very gently, but with a keen edge: it is possible for me, as a Christian, to bring forth the child of someone else instead of my rightful lover, instead of my bridegroom. That is, to bring forth into the external world the fruit of the devil. As an illustration, imagine a married couple of one race, both of the one color of skin. Suddenly, the wife brings forth a child clearly of another race. All the world would know that she had been unfaithful to her proper mate. So it is with us. If I as a Christian am not bringing forth the fruit that one would expect, the fruit of Christ, there is spiritual unfaithfulness on my part. There is spiritual adultery in my life. And when we see it this way, the word *unfaithful* takes on a very special and clear significance, for faith is the instrument by which we bear the fruit of our risen Christ. So the word *faithless* has a very pointed meaning. If I do not have faith toward Christ, I am unfaithful toward him, and this *is* faithlessness.

Now to go on to the third step in my new relationship. When I have accepted Christ as my Savior, I am also immediately in a new relationship to the Holy Spirit. The Holy Spirit lives in me as the agent of the whole Trinity. Now the fruit of the Spirit is clearly delineated in the Bible: "But the fruit of the Spirit is love, joy, peace, longsuffering, gentleness, goodness, faith, meekness, temperance: against such there is no law" (Galatians 5:22-23).

The Scripture is equally clear about the works of the flesh: "Now the works of the flesh are manifest, which are these: Adultery, fornication, uncleanness, lasciviousness, idolatry, witchcraft, hatred, variance, emulations, wrath, strife, seditions, heresies, envyings, murders, drunkenness, revellings, and such like" (Galatians 5:19-21).

The Holy Spirit is the agent of the whole Trinity. He is the agent of the crucified, the raised, the glorified Christ. If I am bringing forth something other than the fruit of the Spirit, the only reason is that I have grieved the Holy Spirit who is our divine guest. Dr. Charles Hodge expresses it like this: "The great distinction of a true Christian is the indwelling of the Holy Spirit. How careful should he be, lest anything in his thoughts or feelings would be offensive to this Divine Guest!" The Holy Spirit is a person, but knowing that he is a person should remind us that he can be grieved, that he can be made sad. So in Ephesians 4:30 we are told, "And grieve not the Holy Spirit of God, whereby ye are sealed unto the day of redemption."

Do not make sad the divine guest who lives in you. If you are a true Christian, you are sealed by him to the day of redemption. It is by his indwelling that our continuing salvation is guaranteed to us. Let us not grieve him, make him sad.

In 1 Thessalonians 5:19 we have the command: "Quench not the Spirit." When we grieve him, we push aside the one who is the agent to us of the work of Christ for our present life. On the basis of the finished, passive work of Christ—that is, his suffering on the cross—and on the basis of the active obedience of Christ—that is, keeping the law perfectly through his life—the fruits are there. They are there to flow out through the agency of the Holy Spirit through us into the external world. The fruits are normal; not to have them is not to have the Christian life which should be considered usual. There are oceans of grace that wait. Orchard upon orchard waits, vineyard upon vineyard of fruit waits. There is only one reason why they do not flow out through the Christian's life, and that is that the instrumentality of faith is not being used. This is to quench the Holy Spirit. When we sin in this sense, we sin twice: we sin in the sin, and this is terrible, as it is against the law and the character of God himself, our Father; but at the same time we sin by omission, because we have not raised the empty hands of faith for the gift that is there.

In the light of the structure of the total universe, in the light of our calling to exhibit the existence and character of God between the Ascension and the Second Coming, in the light of the terrible price of the Cross, whereby all the present and future benefits of salvation were purchased on our behalf—in the light of all this, the real sin of the Christian is not to possess his possessions by faith. This is the *real* sin.

"Whatsoever is not of faith is sin" (Romans 14:23). The sin here is in not raising the empty hands of faith. Anything that is not brought forth from faith is sin. When I am not allowing this fruit, which has been purchased at such a price, to flow forth through me, *I am unfaithful,* in the deep sense of not believing God. When we understand this, certainly we must say, "May God forgive us." The Christian life is a thing of joy, but it should also have the understanding of sorrow, if we compare what could be with what is: the poverty, when riches are offered and when we have brought forth the fruit of the Lord's enemy, the devil, instead of the fruit of our lover, our Lord.

There are two main reasons why we may not be bringing forth the fruit we should. It may be because of ignorance, because we may never have been taught the meaning of the work of Christ for our present lives. There are five possible "ignorances" in this area. *First,* the Christian may have been taught how to be justified but never taught the *present* meaning of the work of Christ for him. *Second,* he may have been taught to become a Christian through the instrumentality of faith, but then he may have been left, as though from that point on the Christian life has to be lived in his own strength. *Third,* he may have been taught the opposite; that is, he may have been taught that, having accepted Christ, in some antinomian way it does not now matter how he lives. *Fourth,* he may have been taught some kind of second blessing, which would make him perfect in this life when he receives it. This the Bible does not teach. And therefore, he just waits hopelessly or tries to act upon that which is not. *Fifth,* he may never have been taught that there is a reality of faith *to be acted on consciously* after justification. This last point is the point of ignorance of many who stand in the orthodox and historic stream of the Reformation.

Because of any of these ignorances, the Christian may not "possess his possessions" in this present life. But when a man does learn the meaning of the work of Christ in the present life, a new door is open to him. And this new door then seems to be so wonderful that often it gives the Christian, as he begins to act upon the knowledge of faith, the sense of something that is as new as was his conversion. And it has been true for many of us that at a certain point, after we have been Christians for a long time, suddenly through the teaching of the Bible—directly or through someone teaching us—we have seen the meaning of the work of Christ and the blood of Jesus Christ for our present life, and a new door opens for us. So what is needed is the knowledge of the meaning of the work of Christ in our present life, for our present life, and then for us to act upon it in faith.

However, we may know the doctrine by mental assent without making the doctrine ours, and that is the other reason we do not bring forth the fruit that we should. In the last analysis it is never doctrine *alone* that is important. It is always doctrine *appropriated* that counts. We can see this in the case of justification. There are many men, unhappily, who have heard the gospel and know the gospel but do not take Christ as their Savior. In such a case a man has the knowledge, but it means nothing to him because he has not taken it. It may be so with us in this matter of our present life. We may know the truth, we may have the knowledge, but it has not been appropriated, and so it will not mean anything to us in practice, and the fruit will not be born. But we do not need to be either ignorant or confused. If we are truly Christians, we know how we were justified when we became Christians. The practice of sanctification is very much parallel to what we know from justification. In other words, if I am a Christian at all, I have been justified, and thinking back to my justification, all I have to do is to see the parallelism between justification and the Christian life. When I see these, there is no reason either to be ignorant or confused, because there are these very definite parallels.

In justification the basis is the finished work of Jesus Christ; in sanctification it is the finished work of Christ. In justification, we must see, acknowledge, and act upon the fact that we cannot save ourselves. In sanctification, we must see, acknowledge, and act upon the fact that we cannot live the Christian life in our own strength, or in our own goodness.

In justification the instrument by which we receive the free gift of God is faith, which believes God as he has given us his promises in the Bible; in sanctification the instrument by which we receive the free gift of God is faith, which believes God as he has given us his promises in the Bible. It is exactly the same thing. There is one difference between the practice of justification and sanctification. As justification deals with our guilt, and sanctification deals with the problem of the power of sin in our lives as Christians, justification is once for all, and the Christian life is *moment by moment*. There is a difference in that one deals with the *guilt* of my sin, and the other deals with the *power* of sin in my life.

If we are Christians, we have understood and acted upon the finished work of Christ once for all at our justification, and our guilt is gone for ever. Now let us understand and act upon the practice of that same work moment by moment in our present lives.

Let me repeat: the only difference in the practice is that in justification it is once for all, and the Christian life is lived moment by moment. The Christian life is acting moment by moment on the same principle, and in the same way, as I acted at the moment of my justification.

But let us notice that from another perspective, even at this point it is not really different, because life is only a succession of moments, one moment at a time. When we say "moment by moment," we are dealing in practice with a succession of single, historical moments. No one lives his whole life at a time. This is another of these places where the existentialists have made a very accurate observation. Life is not a once-for-all thing; it is a series of moments. So when I talk about living the Christian life moment by moment, I can only live it in practice one moment at a time, just as my justification took place in one moment. There is no other way to do it. In this sense, the difference is not absolute between the two. Nobody can live except moment by moment, and only one moment at a time. History is like a knife-edge, razor sharp. God has made sequence to be real, and the present is the present to me, the future is the future, and the past is the past.

So we must believe God's promises at this one moment in which we are. Consequently, in believing God's promises, we apply them—the present meaning of the work of Christ for the Christian—for and in *this one moment*. If you only can see that, everything changes. As we believe God for this moment, the Holy Spirit is not quenched. And through his agency, the risen and glorified Christ, as the Bridegroom of the bride, the Vine, brings forth his fruit through us *at this moment*. This is the practice of *active passivity*. And it is the only way anybody can live; there is no other way to live but moment by moment.

In speaking of active passivity we may again use Mary as an example. Mary, who had the angel's promise that she was to bring forth the long-promised Messiah, believed God and put herself as a bond servant in the hands of God, for him to use her body in bringing forth the baby Jesus, virgin-born. She was passive in that she could not cause the birth of the child, but she was active in that in faith she was obedient and gave herself to God. Now then, notice that she did this in a moment. It does not follow that Mary was always faithful. As a matter of fact, as we read the Gospels, there is good reason to be sure that later she was not always in the same condition of active passivity as she was at that one moment when she said: "Be it unto me according to thy word" (Luke 1:38).

So for Mary, too, it was at that one moment. And so it must be for us. We accept Christ as Savior at one moment and our guilt is gone on the basis of the value of the finished work of Jesus Christ. But after we become Christians, the moments proceed, the clock continues to tick; and in every moment of time, our calling is to believe God, raise the empty hands of faith, and let fruit flow out through us.

Now we have spoken of faith, so let us pause here. Living in the second half of the twentieth century, we must keep on saying what faith is, in the biblical sense. Christian faith is never faith in faith. Christian faith is never without content. Christian faith is never a jump in the dark. Christian faith is always believing what God has said. And Christian faith rests upon Christ's finished work on the cross.

The reality of living by faith as though we were already dead, of living by faith in open communion with God, and then stepping back into the external world as though we are already raised from the dead, this is not once for all, it is a matter of moment-by-moment faith, and living moment by moment. This morning's faith will never do for this noon. The faith of this noon will never do for suppertime. The faith of suppertime will never do for the time of going to bed. The faith of midnight will never do for the next morning. Thank God for the reality for which we were created, a moment-by-moment communication with God himself. We should indeed be thankful because the moment-by-moment quality brings the whole thing to the size which we are, as God has made us.

This being the case, it is obvious that there is no mechanical solution to true spirituality or the true Christian life. Anything that has the mark of the mechanical upon it is a mistake. It is not possible to say, "Read so many of the chapters of the Bible every day, and you will have this much sanctification." It is not possible to say, "Pray so long every day, and you will have a certain amount of sanctification." It is not possible to add the two together and to say, "You will have this big a piece of sanctification." This is a purely mechanical solution, and it denies the whole Christian position. For the fact is that the Christian life, true spirituality, can never have a mechanical solution. The real solution is being cast up into the moment-by-moment communion, personal communion, with God himself, and letting Christ's truth flow through me through the agency of the Holy Spirit.

Let us notice the place to which we have come. It is precisely what we would expect in the light of the total unity of the Bible's most basic teaching. The most basic teaching of the Bible is that God exists, and what he is, and the corollary of what man is as made in God's own image. We live in a personal universe, and not in an impersonal one. God exists, God is personal; we are personal, as we have been made in the image of God, and our relationship to God is to be personal, not mechanical. We are not machines, we are not plants, we are not mere animals, but men, created in the image of God—rational and moral. When we were created, we were created for a purpose And the purpose of our creation, in which all our subsidiary purposes fit, is to be in a personal relationship to God, in communion with him, in love, by choice, the creature before the Creator.

But sin destroyed this. The creature tried to be on the same level as the Creator; the finite sought to be placed on the same level as the infinite. And now, when we are saved on the basis of the finished work of Christ, our guilt is gone and we are returned to this proper relationship, not in a mechanical sense, but in a personal relationship of communion.

So modern man is struggling properly when he is struggling with this basic question, as to the problem of personality and communication. According to the Scripture, this struggle is at the right point: not the point of a few superficial taboos, a few superficial conformities, but of the tremendous problem of personality. The Bible's answer to the problem is that the central communication that makes all the other communications meaningful is the communication of the Creator and the creature, which is restored when I have accepted Christ as my Savior and my guilt is gone.

When this has happened, I am not supposed to set up a rival center in the universe all over again. That would be contrary to the whole thing. When I have accepted Christ as my Savior, I am to be in my appointed position, in the proper place and in a personal relationship with God. This is that for which we were made in the first place. The only difference between our relationship with God now, and that which man's would have been if he had not sinned, is that now it is under the covenant of grace, and not under the covenant of works; therefore, it rests on the basis of Christ's finished mediatorial work. That is the only difference.

On man's side, it is redeemed man as a unity who now stands before the personal God. It is not just one part of man. The will, the mind, the emotions—all are involved: the complete man, as a unit, involved in this moment by moment, one moment at a time, believing God's promises about the significance of the work of Christ in our present lives. Eve doubted God; that was her sin. She called God a liar. Eve doubted God, and I as a child of God am now to do exactly the opposite: I am to believe him. Eve doubted, and mankind in revolt doubts God. To believe him, not just when I accept Christ as Savior, but also at every moment, one moment at a time: this is the Christian life, and this is true spirituality.

FREEDOM NOW FROM THE RESULTS OF THE BONDS OF SIN

CHAPTERS 8-13

CHAPTER 8

FREEDOM FROM CONSCIENCE

In the first seven chapters we considered freedom in the present life from the bonds of sin. Now we turn to consider the question of freedom in the present life from the *results* of the bonds of sin. Or we could call it "Wider Considerations of the True Christian Life." At this point we begin to come into very sharp conflict with the intellectual thinking of the second half of the twentieth century, and we will see what Christianity has to say to this.

With this chapter we begin our consideration with the question of "true spirituality" in relation to my separation *from myself,* which is a result of the fall and a result of sin. *Now we must keep this in the right order.* We must not get it reversed. The sin causes the bondage and the results. Sin causes the bondage, and not the other way round. So the comprehension of and acting upon the freedom from the bonds of sin must be seen as basic and before the consideration of the freedom from the *results* of those bonds of sin. We cannot have the biblical answer, the promises God makes, to the Christian concerning freedom from the results of the bonds of sin in this present life until two things are true: first, that we are truly Christians; and second, that we are acting upon the biblical teaching concerning freedom from the bonds of sin. That is why the first seven chapters of this book must be the base of that which we begin to consider now.

Any meaning becomes only a psychological trick, a cruel illusion, unless certain things are true—objectively true—or are propositional truths, to use the twentieth-century terminology. What are these facts that must be objectively true?

The first of them is the objective reality of a supernatural view of the universe, and the reality of salvation in the biblical sense. Without these, modern man's effort to reach out and scoop some of the blessing off the top of Scripture, as it were, can be no more than a psychological trick. But behind this truth, there stands a yet more basic truth: the existence of a personal-infinite God in whose image man is made. And as we have been created by him, in his image, there is a reality to the concept of human personality. This is in contrast to all deterministic concepts, which say that we are merely a set of psychological or chemical conditions.

The third thing that must be understood is the truth about the human dilemma. The biblical answer is that the dilemma of the human race, this dilemma that twentieth-century man is wrestling with so much, is *moral*. The basic problem of the human race is sin and guilt—a real moral guilt, not just guilt feelings, and a real moral sin, because we have sinned against a God who is there and a God who is holy. In opposition to neoorthodoxy and all the other modern theologies, we must understand that sin and guilt really are moral. They are not simply due to certain metaphysical or psychological limitations. Man is really guilty before a holy God who exists and against whom we have sinned. Except on these bases, the hope given by Scripture concerning freedom from the bonds of sin is only a cruel illusion.

At this point we should consider the question of freedom from my conscience. There are two attitudes which the Word of God and the study of church history warn us against if we are to avoid mistakes. The first one is perfectionism, as it has been called theologically. This is the teaching that a Christian can be perfect in this life. This view falls into two areas. The first is the teaching, sincerely held by many, that at a certain point in a man's life there comes some second blessing, after which he never sins again. The early Wesley taught this—not the later Wesley, for he began to see that this could not be consistently held. But there is another form of perfectionism, which holds that we may know perfection *for the moment*. As we have seen, it is true that our lives are lived on a moment-by-moment basis; this view talks of a moment-by-moment total moral "victory."

Now the question arises whether we could expect to have perfection, either totally or even for this one moment. And I would suggest that such an expression simply gets us caught in a swamp, in which we have endless discussions concerning some abstract idea of complete victory, even in this one moment. The phrase that often is used is that we can have freedom from "all known sin." But I feel that as we consider first the Word of God and then human experience, we must understand that there is a problem in the word "known," and also a problem in the word "conscious," if we talk of "conscious" sin. The problem in using either or both of these words is the fact that since the fall, man has habitually fooled himself. We fool ourselves deep inside our subconscious and unconscious nature.

The more the Holy Spirit puts his finger on my life and goes down deep into my life, the more I understand that there are deep wells to my nature. Modern psychology has dealt with these under the terms unconscious and subconscious, and though the philosophy behind modern psychology is often fundamentally wrong, surely it is right in pointing out that we are more than merely that which is on the surface. We are like the iceberg: one-tenth above and nine-tenths below. It is a very, very simple thing to fool ourselves, and that is why we must question this word "known." If I say I can have freedom from all "known" sin, surely I must acknowledge the meaningfulness of the question: *What do I know?* Until I can describe what I know, I cannot go on meaningfully to ask whether I can have freedom from "known" sin. As the Holy Spirit has wrestled with me down through the years, more and more I am aware of the depths of my own nature, and the depths of the results of that awful fall in the Garden of Eden. Man is separated from himself.

Now we must understand, too, in the framework of the Scripture, that since the Fall everything is under the covenant of grace. The covenant of works is destroyed by the deliberate, free, unconditioned choice of Adam and Eve. In its place, by the grace of God, with the promises begun in Genesis 3:15, man was immediately given the promise of the work of the Messiah, coming in the future. Thus from the time of the Fall onwards, everything rests upon the finished work of the Lord Jesus Christ on the cross, not upon ourselves, not *in* ourselves. Hence if there is any real victory in my life, it must not be thought of as *my* victory or *my* perfection. Such a notion does not fit the scriptural picture of man or God's dealing with us since man has sinned. It is not my victory, it is always Christ's victory; it is never my work or holiness, it is always Christ's work and Christ's holiness. When I begin to think and to grow in the idea of my victory, there is really no true victory. To the extent that I am thinking about *my* sanctification, there is no real sanctification. I must see it always as Jesus Christ's.

Indeed, it is only as we consciously bring each victory to his feet, and keep it there as we think of it—and especially as we speak of it—that we can avoid the pride of that victory, which can be worse than the sin over which we claim to have had the victory. The greater the victory, the greater the need of placing it consciously (and as we speak of it, vocally) at his feet.

We have said that there are two false attitudes against which we must stand, and not just one. The second is just as mistaken as the first.

In the Westminster Catechism there is the emphasis that we sin daily in thought, word, and deed. This is not wrong, but it can be distorted by our sinful hearts into something which is exceedingly wrong. As we teach our children that we sin daily in thought, word, and deed, we must be very careful to warn them of the danger of thinking that they can look lightly or abstractly at sin in their lives. If I count on Christ's victory for my entrance to heaven, will I deny him the glory he would gain in victories won, in me and through me, in my present life? If I look to Jesus Christ and his victory on the cross for my entrance into a future heaven, dare I deny to him what that victory should produce in the battles of the present life—the battles before men and angels and the supernatural world? What an awful thought!

The Bible makes a clear distinction between temptation and sin. Christ was tempted in every point like as we are, yet, the Bible says with great emphasis, he never sinned (Hebrews 4:15). Consequently, there is a difference between temptation and sin, and the Bible says that just because we are tempted does not mean that we must follow through in that temptation and fall into sin.

> There hath no temptation taken you but such as is common to man: but God is faithful, who will not suffer you to be tempted above that ye are able; but will with the temptation also make a way to escape, that ye may be able to bear it. (1 Corinthians 10:13)

> For this is the love of God, that we keep his commandments: and his commandments are not grievous. For whatsoever is born of God overcometh the world: and this is the victory that overcometh the world, even our faith. (1 John 5:3-4)

It is not we who overcome the world in our own strength. We do not have a power plant inside ourselves that can overcome the world. The overcoming is the work of the Lord Jesus Christ, as we have already seen. There can be a victory, a practical victory, if we raise the empty hands of faith moment by moment and accept the gift. "This is the victory that overcometh the world." God has promised, and the Bible has said, that there is a way to escape temptation. By God's grace we should want that escape.

Having spoken of these two dangers, let us go on.

Let us say now that I have been living in the light of what God has been giving us for the present life. As a born-again child of God, I have been practicing the reality of true spirituality, as Christ has purchased it for us. *And then sin reenters.* For some reason my moment-by-moment belief in God falters—a fondness for some specific sin has caused me at that point not to draw in faith upon the fact of a restored relationship with the Trinity. The *reality* of the practice of true spirituality suddenly slips from me. I look up some morning, some afternoon, some night—and something is gone, something I have known: my quietness and my peace are gone. It is not that I am lost again, because justification is once for all. But as far as man can see, or even I myself, at this point there is no exhibition of the victory of Christ upon the cross. Looking at me at this point, men would see no demonstration that God's creation of moral rational creatures is not a complete failure, or even that God exists. Because God still holds me fast, I do not have the separation of lostness, but I do have the separation from my Father in the parent-child relationship. *And I remember what I had.*

At this point a question must arise: Is there a way back? Or is it like a fine Bavarian porcelain cup, dropped to a tile floor so that it is smashed beyond repair?

Thank God, the gospel includes this. The Bible is always realistic; it is not romantic, but deals with realism—with what I am. There is a way back, and the basis of the way back is nothing new to us. The basis is again the blood of Christ, the finished work of the Lamb of God: the once-for-all completed work of Christ upon the cross, in space, time, and history.

And the first step of the way back is not new either. No man is justified, no man becomes a Christian, until he acknowledges he is a sinner. No man can accept Jesus as Savior until he acknowledges he is a sinner. And 1 John 1:4-9 makes it plain that the first step in the restoration of the Christian after he has sinned is to admit to God that what he has done is sin. He must not excuse it; he must not call it by another name; he must not blame it upon somebody else; he must not call it less than sin. He must be sorry for it.

And these things write we unto you, that your joy may be full. This then is the message which we have heard of him, and declare unto you, that God is light, and in him is no darkness at all. If we say that we have fellowship with him, and walk in darkness, we lie, and do not the truth: but if we walk in the light, as he is in the light [and that light is not just a general illumination; it is clearly his holiness], *we have fellowship one with another, and the blood of Jesus Christ his Son cleanseth us from all sin* [a present cleansing]. *If we say that we have no sin, we deceive ourselves, and the truth is not in us. If we confess our sins, he is faithful and just to forgive us our sins, and to cleanse us from all unrighteousness. (1 John 1:4-9)*

This is the gentle dealing of God with his children after we have fallen. This is the purpose of God's chastisement of the Christian; it is to cause us to acknowledge that the specific sin is sin.

And ye have forgotten the exhortation which speaketh unto you as unto children, My son, despise not thou the chastening of the Lord, nor faint when thou art rebuked of him: for whom the Lord loveth he chasteneth, and scourgeth every son whom he receiveth. If ye endure chastening, God dealeth with you as with sons; for what son is he whom the father chasteneth not? But if ye be without chastisement, whereof all are partakers, then are ye bastards, and not sons. (Hebrews 12:5-8)

If we have sin in our lives, and we go on, and God does not put his hand in loving chastisement upon us, then we are not children of God. God loves us too much for that. He loves us tremendously. He loves us as his adopted children.

Furthermore we have had fathers of our flesh which corrected us, and we gave them reverence: shall we not much rather be in subjection unto the Father of spirits, and live? For they verily for a few days chastened us after their own pleasure [as seemed good to them]; but he for our profit, that we might be partakers of his holiness. Now no chastening for the present seemeth to be joyous, but grievous: nevertheless afterward it yieldeth the peaceable fruit of righteousness unto them which are exercised thereby. (Hebrews 12:9-11)

He does all this for a purpose. It is not only to bring righteousness into my life, but it is also that I might have that "peaceable fruit of righteousness"—that these things being dealt with, I may be at peace. That is God's loving care.

But there is a condition to it. Those who have this peaceable fruit of righteousness are those who are exercised by God's chastening: in other words, learning what he is teaching them in the midst of it. God the Father's chastening is to cause us to acknowledge that a specific sin is sin; his hand can grow increasingly heavy until we come to acknowledge that it is sin and stop trying to get out from under it through fancy terms, blaming it on other people or excusing it in some way. Do we want a restored relationship? We may have it, as children of God. We may have a restored relationship any moment, but we are not ready for it until we are willing to call specific sin *sin*.

And the emphasis is on *specific* sin. It will not do just to say, "I sinned." This is nothing. There must be a willingness to call my specific sin *sin*. I must take my place in the Garden of Gethsemane with Christ. There Christ is speaking as a true man, and he speaks the absolute reverse of Adam and Eve in the Garden of the Fall, when he says, "Not my will, but thine be done." I, too, must say with meaningfulness, "Not my will, but thine be done," *at the point of that specific sin;* not just a general statement, "I want your will," but "I want your will in *reference to this thing* that I acknowledge to be sin."

If we say that we have fellowship with him, and walk in darkness, we lie, and do not the truth. (1 John 1:6)

There is no such thing as to continue deliberately to walk in darkness and to have an open fellowship with him who is only light and holiness. This is simply not possible.

For all that is in the world, the lust of the flesh, and the lust of the eyes, and the pride of life, is not of the Father, but is of the world. (1 John 2:16)

Here is something that is the antithesis not only of God's external law, but of his character and what he is. How can we say we have fellowship with him if we deliberately walk in that which is the antithesis of himself?

Thus we say, "Not my will, but thine be done." And as I say this in reference to this specific sin, I am once again the creature before God; I am in the place for which I was made. As a child of the Fall, self is crucified again, for there can be no resurrection without the crucifixion. We have seen that the order of the Christian life is plain: there can be no restitution without repentance and confession directly to God. In the unity of the teaching of Scripture, this is exactly what one would expect if one begins with the central biblical teaching that God really exists. He is a personal-infinite God, and he has a character. He is holy. This is not some strange thing pulled in from a peripheral point; it stands at the very heart of the matter. If this is what God is, the God who exists, and if I have become his child, should one not expect that when I have sinned, when I have done that which is the antithesis of his character, I must go back to him as a person, and say I am sorry? He is not just a doctrine, or an abstraction; he is a person who is there. In practice we may not comprehend all that is involved in the sin and, especially if a person is psychologically disturbed, he may not always be able to sort out what really is sin and what is just confusion on his part. Here is the concept of the iceberg again, the nine-tenths below the surface and only one-tenth above, so that we cannot always sort out all that we are in the midst of our sin. Much of the sin may be below the surface; much may even be in the subconscious boiling up, just showing itself in spots. But whatever evil may be above the surface, the portion that we *do* comprehend *is* sin, and that portion must be taken with honesty before the God who knows our whole being, and we must say to him, "Father, I have sinned." There must be real sorrow for the sin that I know, that is above the surface of myself.

We have seen earlier that there is a parallel between justification and sanctification, that is, between becoming a Christian and living the Christian life. The first step in justification is that I must acknowledge that I am a sinner, that I am justly under the wrath of God, and that I cannot save myself. The first step in living the true Christian life is that I must acknowledge that I cannot live the Christian life in my own strength or in my own goodness. The first step of restoration after I have sinned is in exactly the same line: I must acknowledge that my specific sin is sin. There are not three different principles; there is one principle in these three places, because we are dealing with the same God and basically the same problem. But neither in becoming a Christian, nor in fruit-bearing as a Christian, is the first step enough on its own. In each of the three situations, I must then raise the hands of faith for God's gift in that place. And when I, a Christian, have sinned, it is only the finished work of Jesus Christ in space, time, and *history*, back there on Calvary's cross, that is enough. It is only the blood of Jesus Christ that is enough to cleanse my sin as a Christian, and it is only upon the basis of the blood of Christ that the spot is removed. I must bring the specific sin under the blood of Jesus Christ, by faith. So it is the same thing again; here is the active passivity which we have already discussed. We cannot do it of ourselves, but neither are we sticks or stones. God has made us in his own image, and he will always deal with us on that ground.

Now just as in the conscious area of sanctification as a whole, so here in restoration: everything rests upon the reality of the fact that the blood of Christ has meaning in *our present life,* and restoration takes place as we, in faith, act upon that fact in specific cases of sin. I think that much of the emphasis of the traditional, orthodox church in the historic stream of the Reformation has laid insufficient stress on the conscious side of the Christian life. This is *not* a "second blessing," but it is learning the reality of the meaning of the work of Jesus Christ on the cross, in our present life, and consciously beginning to act upon it.

I think this is what John Wesley knew. He knew a direct working of God in his life on the basis of the finished work of Jesus Christ. I think his theology in this area was mistaken, and he used the wrong terminology, but certainly he did not have the wrong aspiration, but the right one: the knowledge and practice of the availability of the blood of the Lord Jesus Christ in the present meaning of our life. No matter what terms we use to express it, the reality of it rests upon the knowledge of what Christ has purchased for us—not only in taking us to heaven, but in the present life—and then beginning to act upon this in moment-by moment faith.

And in the question of restoration: the blood of Christ has meaning for me in my present life when I have fallen and my peace is gone. Restoration must be first upon the *understanding* of what Christ has done for us in this area, and then beginning to practice this moment by moment. It is not a mechanical process; the meaning of the work of Christ in our present life is to be consciously acted upon. But the base is the finished work of Christ in history.

How glad we should be for Christ's story of the Prodigal Son. Here is one who is a son and yet has gone deeply into sin, down into the mire. Scripture makes it plain that he has not just sinned a little, even in the world's view of sin. He has sinned the "big" sins. Yet the father stands waiting when the prodigal returns, his arms ready to close about him. The blood of Christ can cleanse the darkest sin. There is no sin so great that our fellowship cannot be restored, if we humbly call it sin and, through faith, bring that specific sin under the blood of Christ. When my heart condemns me and cries, "You have done it again," I am to believe God again as to the value of the finished work of Jesus Christ. There must be death, we have seen, before there can be resurrection. But on the basis of the victory of Christ, resurrection should follow death. The Christian life never ends on the negative. There *is* a negative, because man is a rebel. But it does not end there; it always goes on to the positive. As my body will one day be raised from the dead, so I am meant to live a resurrected life now.

I have found it extremely helpful that when a man has accepted Christ as his Savior, he should bow his head and say "Thank you" to the God who is there—"Thank you for the completed work." Undoubtedly men have been saved and have gone away not consciously saying "Thank you" but how wonderful it is when a man has seen himself as a sinner, and has understood his lostness, for that man to have accepted Christ as his Savior and then to have bowed his head consciously to say "Thank you" for a work that is *absolute* and *complete*. It is usually when the newly-born one thanks God that the assurance comes, that he comes to rest in certainty and in peace.

It is the same in restoration. There is a continuing parallel here. If we have sinned, it is wonderful consciously to say, "Thank you for a completed work," after we have brought that specific sin under the finished work of Christ. While not absolutely necessary for restoration, the conscious giving of thanks brings assurance and peace. We say "Thank you" for work completed upon the cross, which is sufficient for a completely restored relationship. This is not on the basis of my emotions, any more than in my justification. The basis is the finished work of Christ in history and the objective promises of God in the written Word. If I believe him, and if I believe what he has taught me about the sufficiency of the work of Christ for restoration, I can have assurance, no matter how black the blot has been, This is the Christian reality of salvation from one's conscience.

Martin Luther, in his commentary on Galatians, shows a great understanding of the fact that our salvation includes salvation from the bondage of our conscience. It is, of course, natural and right that as we become Christians our consciences should become ever more tender. This is a work of the Holy Spirit. However, I should not be bowed down by my conscience year after year over sins that are past. When my conscience under the Holy Spirit makes me aware of a specific sin, I should at once call that sin *sin* and bring it consciously under the blood of Christ. Now it is covered, and it is not honoring to the finished work of Jesus Christ to worry about it, as far as my relationship to God is concerned. Indeed, to worry about it is to do despite to the infinite value of the death of the Son of God. My fellowship with God *is* restored.

Now there may be a price yet to pay for my sins in regard to the state;

there may be a harm to individuals that I have to deal with. These things still have to be faced. We will consider this later. But as far as my fellowship with the Father is concerned, God says it is restored upon the basis of the value of the blood of Jesus Christ. And if his blood is of such a value as to bring a rebel and a sinner from the kingdom of darkness to the kingdom of God's dear Son at justification, what sin is so black that it cannot cover it?

As I consciously say "Thank you" to God for a *completed work*, my conscience should come into rest.

For myself, through the twenty years or so since I began to struggle with this in my own life, I rather picture my conscience as a big black dog with enormous paws which leaps upon me, threatening to cover me with mud and devour me. But as this conscience of mine jumps upon me, after a specific sin has been dealt with on the basis of Christ's finished work, then I should turn to my conscience and say, in effect, "Down! Be still!" I am to believe God and be quiet in my practice and experience. My fellowship with God has been supernaturally restored. I am cleansed, ready again to resume the spiritual life, ready again to be used by the Spirit for warfare in the external world. I cannot be ready until I am cleansed, but when I am, then I am ready. And I may come back for cleansing as many times as I need, on this basis.

This is for many Christians the point of reality. All of us battle with this problem of reality. Men go to strange extremes to touch reality, but here is the point of it: "My little children, these things write I unto you, that ye sin not [so naturally the call is not to sin]. And if any man sin, we [including John himself, who puts himself in this category] have an advocate with the Father, Jesus Christ the righteous" (1 John 2:1).

This is the point of reality for me personally. If I lay hold upon the blood of Christ in faith, reality rests here, not in trying to live as though the Bible teaches perfectionism. That is no basis for reality; that is only a basis either for subterfuge or despair. But there is reality here: the reality of sins forgiven; the reality of a certainty that when a specific sin is brought under the blood of our Lord Jesus Christ, it is forgiven. This is the reality of restored relationship. Reality is not meant to be only credal, though the creeds are important. Reality is to be experienced, and experienced on the basis of a restored relationship with God through that finished work of the Lord Jesus Christ on the cross.

One thing more needs to be said on this subject: "For if we would judge ourselves, we should not be judged. But when we are judged, we are chastened of the Lord, that we should not be condemned with the world" (1 Corinthians 11:31-32).

This teaches us that we do not need to wait to be chastened before our fellowship with God can be restored. God's chastening is not a punishment. The punishment is altogether dealt with on Calvary's cross. It is a correction to bring us back to fellowship with himself, and we do not need to wait to be chastened before our fellowship can be restored. The chastening of a child of God does not have a penal aspect. That was finished on the cross. There is no double jeopardy when the holy God is the Judge. Our guilt is gone, once and forever. Therefore if we judge ourselves, we are not chastened.

Consequently we may read these two verses backwards. And that is, God is not going to have us condemned with the world, so he will chasten us. But if we judge ourselves, and call the sin sin, and bring it under the blood of the Lord Jesus Christ, then he will not have to chasten us. This is what Paul was urging upon us. It is overwhelmingly better not to sin. But is it not wonderful that when we do sin, we can hurry to the place of restoration?

So God means us to have, as one of his gifts in this life, freedom from a false tyranny of the conscience. Most, if not all, Christians find that the first step in the substantial healing that they can have in the present life is the substantial healing of the separation from themselves that is a result of the Fall and of sin. Man is first of all separated from God, then from himself, and finally from his fellow men and from nature. The blood of the Lord Jesus Christ will give an absolute and perfect restoration of all these things when Jesus comes. But in the present life there is to be a substantial healing, including the results of the separation between a man and himself. This is the first step towards freedom in the present life from the results of the bonds of sin.

CHAPTER 9

FREEDOM IN THE THOUGHT-LIFE

The next step is to discuss true spirituality in relation to separation from ourselves in the internal world of thought.

In Romans 1:22-29, we find an order established. Introductory to this passage we notice in verse 21: "Because that, when they knew God, they glorified him not as God, neither were thankful; but became vain in their imaginations, and their foolish heart was darkened."

Here are those who knew God. We can think of it in terms of the original fall of Adam and Eve, or we can think of it in terms of those many, many times when a culture has known the true God and has deliberately turned away, as is the case in our own post-Christian world. We see that they knew God, but they became vain in their reasoning. This is the world of their thoughts. Then, in verse 22: "Professing themselves to be wise, they became fools." This is an internal thing; the external is in verse 24: "Wherefore God also gave them up to uncleanness through the lusts of their own hearts, to dishonour their own bodies between themselves." This is the result. Thus we see the order: first there was an idea in their thought-life, and then came the outward result of the idea.

In verse 25 we are told that they "changed the truth of God into a lie, and worshipped and served the creature [created thing] more than the Creator." Here is the inward rebellion, and immediately this brought external results as we saw in verse 24.

Look now at verse 28: "And even as they did not like to retain God in their knowledge, God gave them over to a reprobate mind [that is, a mind void of judgment], to do those things which are not convenient [becoming]." Here again is the same order. Beginning with the twenty-ninth verse, we go through an awful list of the outward things.

We can say two things about the external act: the external follows the internal, and the external is a product of the internal. Thoughts are first, and they produce the external. This is the order.

I beseech you therefore, brethren, by the mercies of God, that ye present your bodies a living sacrifice, holy, acceptable unto God, which is your reasonable service. (Romans 12:1)

Now this is in the external world. But notice this cannot be separated from verse 2:

And be not conformed to this world: but be ye transformed by the renewing of your mind, that ye may prove what is that good, and acceptable, and perfect, will of God.

There is indeed to be a presenting of our bodies, but this has meaning only on the basis of the understanding of the internal.

Paul speaks here of not being conformed to this world. But that is not simply externally. In contrast to this, we are to be transformed by the renewing of our mind, and that is internal.

In Ephesians 4:17 Paul writes: "This I say therefore, and testify in the Lord, that ye henceforth walk not as other Gentiles walk, in the vanity of their mind." Here is the Gentile world, the lost world. They are walking "in the vanity of their mind." Surely this sounds like Romans 1: "They became vain in their reasonings." This is an inward thing. This is what is wrong with the Gentile world: the vanity of its mind.

In Ephesians 4:18 we are given the reason for this: "Having the understanding darkened, being alienated from the life of God through the ignorance that is in them, because of the blindness [or hardness] of their hearts." So we are told that their understanding is darkened; that is an internal thing. All of this flows from the basis of their rebellion against God. It is exactly as Romans 1 explains it. But after showing where "the Gentiles" stand, there comes verse 19, with its picture of men "past feeling," giving themselves over to "lasciviousness [licentiousness], to work all uncleanness and greediness." So again the order is the same: the internal, then the external.

Now we are brought sharply to a contrast in verse 20: "But ye have not so learned Christ." The word "learned," let us notice, is again an internal thing.

This is exactly parallel to Romans 12, where in verse 2 we read "by the renewing of your mind." That is an internal thing, and so is this. But Ephesians 4:22 is the outward: "That ye put off concerning the former conversation the old man, which is corrupt according to the deceitful lusts."

The "conversation" here encompasses the whole set of life. It is in itself an internal aspect. Then it flows over into the external. So this all rests upon verse 20, "Ye have not so learned Christ," which is an internal thing. The internal thing has internal motion from it: first to internal results, and then to external results.

Now you will notice here another element in this that is most important in the twentieth century, and in the midst of twentieth-century thinking. In verse 18 it speaks of ignorance. Ignorance is in relationship to content; it is not just a spirit of ignorance. In verse 21 it speaks of "the truth in Jesus." Truth is content, truth has something to do with reason. Truth has something to do with the rational creature that God has made us. The dilemma here in the internal world is not just some sort of gray fog, it is in relationship to content.

"Be renewed in the spirit of your mind" (verse 23). This again is not simply a feeling. It is a matter of thoughts in a rational sense, and with content. "That ye put on the new man which after God is created in righteousness and [the best translation here is] holiness of truth" (Ephesians 4:24).

This is not just an emotional holiness but holiness in relationship to content, holiness in relationship to thought and a set of things that can be stated as true, in contrast to that which is false. What is being dealt with here is the problem of internal ignorance in the sense of rebellion, turning from those things that are truth.

Here are inward thoughts: thoughts in relationship to specific content, leading on to the external. In Ephesians 5:15-16 there is a parallel passage: "See then that ye walk circumspectly, not as fools, but as wise, redeeming the time, because the days are evil."

The word "wise" here conveys the same message. It has to do with the thought-world, but in contact with that which can be stated as true: "Wherefore be ye not unwise, but understanding what the will of the Lord is" (verse 17). "Unwise" is in contrast to "wise" and "understanding." "Understanding" is again in the thought-world, in relationship to what the will of the Lord is. The "will of the Lord" here is not an existential notion in the twentieth-century sense. It is concerned with content again, in relationship to what we would speak of as propositional or objective truth. In contrast to "walking foolishly" there is verse 18: "And be not drunk with wine, wherein is excess; but be filled with the Spirit."

Verses 19-21 begin to set out some of the external results of this: "Speaking to yourselves in psalms and hymns and spiritual songs, singing and making melody in your heart to the Lord; giving thanks always for all things unto God and the Father in the name of our Lord Jesus Christ; submitting yourselves one to another in the fear of God."

These are external results of a previously adopted position in the thought-world. There is an additional element here which is most important in our thinking. The work of the Holy Spirit, as the agent of the Trinity, is not a coat we put on. It is not an external thing at all, but internal, bringing, in turn, something external.

So here we move on in our understanding of true spirituality in the Christian life. Basically it is a matter of our *thoughts*. The external is the expression, the results. Moral battles are not won in the external world first. They are always a result flowing naturally from a cause, and the cause is in the internal world of one's thoughts. In fact, Jesus emphasized this with great force: "O generation of vipers, how can ye, being evil, speak good things? For out of the abundance of the heart the mouth speaketh" (Matthew 12:34).

There are those who would make a distinction here and regard "the heart" as more than just thoughts, but even if one held this view, the important fact is simply that here we are dealing with the internal world. What Jesus is saying is that if the internal condition is not right, one cannot bring forth proper results.

"Not that which goeth into the mouth defileth a man; but that which cometh out of the mouth, this defileth a man" (Matthew 15:11). Jesus is talking about the question put to him earlier: "Why do thy disciples transgress the tradition of the elders? for they wash not their hands when they eat bread." This kind of question is very important to the externalist. But Jesus says: Don't you understand something? It is what comes *out* of a man, this is what defiles a man.

> "Do not ye yet understand, that whatsoever entereth in at the mouth goeth into the belly, and is cast out into the draught? But those things which proceed out of the mouth come forth from the heart; and they defile the man. For out of the heart proceed evil thoughts, murders, adulteries, fornications, thefts, false witness, blasphemies: these are the things which defile a man: but to eat with unwashen hands defileth not a man." (Matthew 15:17-20)

Again, it is the internal that Jesus stresses. The internal comes before the external, and the internal produces the external. It is a matter of cause and effect.

In the Sermon on the Mount, Jesus deals with this, too. "Ye have heard that it was said by them of old time, Thou shalt not kill; and whosoever shall kill shall be in danger of the judgment: but I say unto you, That whosoever is angry with his brother without a cause shall be in danger of the judgment" (Matthew 5:21-22).

Compare this with 1 John 3:15: "Whosoever hateth his brother is a murderer." Now we have come a step further. The thought-world is still first, but here we are told something else. In relation to morals, *the thought is the thing*. Hate does not just lead to murder; morally, it *is* murder. Now I am stressing "morally," because that is different from murder in the external world. Nevertheless, morally, the hate *is* the murder.

So far we have taken three steps: first, the internal is first; second, the internal causes the external; third, morally, the internal is central. You will remember that in chapter 1 we saw that any time we break one of the other commandments we have already broken the internal commandment not to covet.

In the story of Joseph, in Genesis 37:4, we have a perfect example of this. "They [Joseph's brothers] hated him and could not speak peaceably unto him." It is the internal hate that is the root of the whole thing. Then: "They hated him yet the more for his dreams, and for his words" (34:8). The hate is piling up, and the hate is an internal thing. Indeed, it has already produced its fruit, in that they cannot speak peaceably with him. And now it is just piling up, like a great wave ready to break. Then: "And his brethren envied him" (34:11).

Here we have the breaking of the commandment not to covet. This is broken now, and internally, the thing is past. As far as the moral situation is concerned, although the total external result has yet to come, the reality of it is already upon them. "And they conspired against him to slay him. . . . Come now therefore, and let us slay him, and cast him into some pit, and we will say, Some evil beast hath devoured him: and we shall see what will become of his dreams" (34:18, 20). They are perfectly willing to kill their brother and break their father's heart. All these things arose in the internal world of their thoughts—in their hatred, in their envy—not in the external world. The sin of the brothers was not when they sold Joseph to Egypt, but in the reality of the internal world. It is the internal world of thought that distinguishes man as man. In the introduction to *The Epic of Man*, Loren Eisley, an anthropologist at the University of Pennsylvania, said this about

99

man: "Ancestral man has entered his own head, and he has been adapting ever since to what he finds there."

This is a most amazing statement, because it is as clear and as sharp as a diamond. It is perfectly true in one portion of it, and perfectly untrue in what he makes of it.

Eisley made this statement into an evolutionary proposition, and here he is wrong, but he is completely right in observing that man, whether one finds him in a more primitive state or in a sophisticated and culturally civilized state, is distinguished as man by the fact that in a very real way he lives inside his own head. He has an internal world of thought that is unique. The modern depth-psychology has the same comprehension. The modern depth-psychology says the thing that distinguishes man from animals is that man—strangely enough for them, for they do not know where this came from—has a fear of non-being. Something "in his head" distinguishes man, not something external. He has a thought-life that is different from anything else we observe in our world. Man lives in his head; this (with verbalization) is the uniqueness of man.

In the account of the fall of man in Genesis 3:6 we read: "And when the woman saw that the tree was good for food, and that it was pleasant to the eyes, and a tree to be desired to make one wise. . . ." Here is the realization that sin is first internal where moral things are concerned. But it has an external result: "She took the fruit thereof, and did eat, and gave also unto her husband with her; and he did eat." The Fall runs from the internal to the external.

But we discover a startling thing in Isaiah 14:13-14—the fall of Satan, prior to the fall of man: "For thou hast said in thine heart, I will ascend into heaven, I will exalt my throne above the stars of God: I will sit also upon the mount of the congregation, in the sides of the north: I will ascend above the heights of the clouds; I will make myself like the most High."

Where did all this take place? First of all, we must realize that Satan is not pictured in the Bible as having a corporeal body such as we have, nor a corporeal heart. This Scripture is talking about things which are internal. Where is the sin of Satan, Lucifer, as he fell? "Thou hast said *in thine heart*." The rebellion of Lucifer, and then of Eve as it followed, is first internal, and then the external flows from it.

But let us come back to Adam and Eve for a moment, in the Fall and in their rebellion. What do we find here? We find Adam—and I speak only of him because it is easier to speak of one—operating as a unit of personality.

His thoughts, his will, and his emotions are all involved as a unit. He is not just a collection of parts. There is a unit that is the individual man, the individual personality, and that is what is in operation here: somebody we can call Adam, or Eve. In each case, we are dealing with a unit of personality.

Now as we deal with the fall of Satan and then with the fall of Adam and Eve, in one sense we must think of them unitedly, for Satan has rebelled before he leads Eve into temptation, and before she in turn gives the fruit to Adam. In terms of what I call "the theology of the Fall," the really vital factor is that there was *no prior conditioning*. What we have is the unit of personality making an absolutely unconditional choice *in the thought-world*. And thus there is here a true first cause. The whole of Christian theology and every Christian answer falls to the ground if we allow previous conditioning to enter in at this point. There is a unit of personality which makes in the thought-world a true choice, which is a true first cause of an external result. It produces something that did not exist before, something terrible, something that has led us to all our tears and all our sorrows: *evil*. God, being infinite, knows all things without experimentation with them. God, being infinite, knows not only all that shall be, but all that *could* be. He does not need to experiment in order to know the possibilities. He has made man and angels and there is a possibility for evil in the universe because God has made them truly moral and really rational. He has made them so that they can love or can say no to love, even against God himself. And here, at the Fall, we have the unit of personality making a true choice in the world of thought, with a true first cause that produced something that flashed like lightning over all the world of man: evil, black, and dark, with a vast sea of tears. They have thought—as a unit of personality—they have chosen, and they have brought forth into the external world.

So here is our next point: from the inside outward they have made something. From the inside outward they have truly made sin.

Now let us think of this in relationship to God. God is spirit. Therefore, he is not corporeal, but he is personal. We see this in Hebrews 11:6, where it says that God "is a rewarder of them that diligently seek him." That which distinguishes the Judeo-Christian God is the concept of God as personal yet infinite. And as a personal God, he thinks, he acts, and he feels. And in the area of creation, God thought, God spoke, and it *was:* a real external world. This is wonderful beyond words. Christian Science is wrong when it makes everything only a thought-world. Eastern thinking is wrong, which very often would reduce everything eventually to a dream of God.

The external world is not an extension of God's essence. The universe is not God; it has a real objective existence. There is a real external existence outside of God, because he made it outside of himself. It is not a part of himself. He spoke and it was, externally and really. Let us notice the Bible's statement that after creation "all things by him *consist*" (Colossians 1:17), all things by him "hang together." The external world which he made is now not a rival center in the universe. By him all things *hang together,* and yet the Bible itself insists that because God made it, it is a real, objective, external world.

But we must not forget the other side, or we forget part of the wonder of what we should know about the world as it is and God as he is. And that is that the thought of the Trinity came first. God said, "Let *us* make man in *our* image" (Genesis 1:26). We are swept back into the Trinity before the creation of the world. Here is thought, because God is a personal God, who thinks, who acts, and who feels in his love. The balances here are most delicate, and we must hold both sides or we lose the wealth of the Christian position. There is an external world; it is not the extension of God's essence. But while there is a true external world which is not the extension of God's essence, God *thought* first. These realities were in the thought of God before they were brought forth by his power, his creative *fiat* as the objective and external world.

On the ceiling of the Sistine Chapel in Rome, there are the tremendous frescoes by Michelangelo. Among them is that magnificent picture of the creation of man. God is reaching out his finger, and man, having just been created, reaches to him as well. But their fingers do not touch. This is a true Christian insight. Man is not an extension of God, cut off like a reproducing amoeba. God created man external to himself, and they must not touch in the picture. Whatever Michelangelo had in mind, surely those who formulated the Chalcedonian Christology in the early creeds of the church had this sharply in mind when they said that even in the one person of Jesus Christ there is no commingling of the human and the divine natures. But there is another part of this fresco of Michelangelo that I would use as an illustration at this present point. The arm of God is thrown backwards and there are two kinds of figures under his arm. There are some little cherub figures that one would take as the Renaissance idea of the representation of angels. But there is another person under his arm: a beautiful girl. Her face is startled, but she is magnificent. And most people have felt that this is a representation of Eve. She is not yet created, but *she is in the mind of God.*

At this point one must say what would be a wrong interpretation of

Michelangelo's painting and what would be right. If he were saying that she was just as "real" in the mind of God as she would be later after he had created her, then that is a non-Christian concept. It is Eastern. Eve became externally, objectively real at that great moment when God put Adam to sleep and made the female from the male. But if Michelangelo meant that before God created Eve he had already thought about her, then this is flamingly true. The thought of God preceded his creative acts.

However, we must make a second point, and it teaches us something about ourselves as well. It is this: That which was created out of nothing and now has objective, external reality does show forth the thought of God, and it is therefore an exhibition of who and what he is. The external world is not an extension of the essence of God; nevertheless, the external world does reveal and exhibit who and what God is. We must hold both sides. There has been a fall, which has marred the created world; nevertheless, Paul reminds us in Romans 1 that man is condemned against the backdrop of the Creation, which, in spite of the Fall, still speaks of God. The external created world is a revelation of God. In theology this is spoken of as the general revelation of God, which surrounds man in the external world, exhibiting God's deity both in the internal nature of man himself, which speaks of God as personal, and in the evidence of the thought of God expressed in the external, created universe.

"General revelation" and "special revelation" are theological terms which deserve some analysis. The Bible is the special revelation. We need the Bible for the message of salvation and for the knowledge it gives that is the "key" to general revelation. But the general revelation—that which God has made and that which we are and that which surrounds us—shows forth the existence of God and gives a true revelation of him. General revelation and special revelation constitute a unified revelation.

Now let us move back to man. All of this is parallel to what the Bible says about us as made in the image of God. The internal thought-world is first, and the internal thought-world causes the external. This should not surprise us, because we have been made in the image of God, and thus are rational and moral. Putting these elements together, we find: God thinks, and then God brings forth into the external world that he had originally created out of nothing; we think, and we bring forth into the external world. God's creation was not an extension of his essence but it does exhibit what he truly is. Equally, our acts in the external world, which spring from our thoughts, are not an extension of our essence, but they do exhibit what we are. The table that is shaped by the carpenter is not an extension of the essence of the carpenter, but it does show something of the essence of the carpenter, out of his thought-world. Satan, Adam, and Eve brought forth evil and brought it forth as a true first cause, each one in his personality, each one acting as a unit. And each one of us, too, created in the image of God, is a true first cause. We are finite, so we cannot create out of nothing; only God creates out of nothing. I am limited, but out of my thought-world I can bring forth, through my body, into the true external world. My body is the bridge into the external world.

Let us notice that this is exactly the reverse of how we are affected by the external world. Something occurs in the outward, external world. I come into contact with this through my senses. It feeds back, through my senses, my body, into my thought-world, and affects me. My senses are the bridge between what happens in the external world and the affecting of the unit that I am, a personality. My body is the bridge. Now it is exactly the same in the opposite direction. My body is the bridge. I think, but when I think, I am able to bring forth, flowing through my fingertips into a true, objective, external world, and I am able to influence and make in that external world. How great is man! We think, and through our bodies the reality flows out into the external world. We do not create out of nothing, as God creates, but in the sense of which we are speaking here it is proper to say that the artist does create and each of us creates. I remember that when I was younger, I was always greatly distressed at the use of the word "create" where the artist, the poet, and the composer are concerned. I thought this word ought to be saved for God. But now that I have thought it through more and have struggled more, I am glad that the word "create" is used. It is perfectly accurate. God's creation and mine differ, of course. God can create out of nothing, by fiat. I cannot, because only he is infinite. In creation, he is limited only by his own character. I am limited not only by my character, but also by my finiteness. When I create, I bring forth in the external universe that he has created. But nevertheless, understanding the limitations and differences, it is perfectly proper to say God creates, and we create.

It can be said that it is impossible for men not to create things constantly and truly. Even if I wished to stop I could not. It is impossible not to be creating things truly and constantly out of my thought-world into the external world and giving them permanent expression. The artist thinks, and he brings his picture forth into the external world. But it was first of all *in his mind*. It is the same for the engineer, for the arranger of flowers, for me writing this book. When we find the creation of a personal being, it has the marks of thought upon it, in contrast to that which pure chance brings forth. There are some borderline cases, of course, such as a stalactite or a piece of driftwood into which we "read" shapes, but almost always when I look at that which I see, I can tell whether it has the mark of personality and thought behind it, or whether it is just a product of mechanical forces. In spite of his theories of chance, we may be sure that when Jacques Monod looks at that which surrounds him, he makes exactly this same kind of judgment in the everyday things of life.

Christian Science and Eastern thinking and philosophical idealism are counterfeits rather than total lies. These philosophies are totally wrong in their system and in their direction, but they are not stupid. The reason they trap man is not that they say nothing, but that they are perversions, they are counterfeits. Although we do not produce an extension of our essence, there is a revelation of ourselves, just as God did not create by an extension of his essence, but what he has created is a revelation of himself. Concerning man there is a body, and there is a real, external world. But the thoughts are first, and they are central. So this is where true spirituality in the Christian life rests: in the realm of my thought-life.

With this perspective, I would like to reexamine various elements of the Christian life, or true spirituality, as we have seen them in the earlier chapters.

First, we have said that in the true Christian life, or true spirituality, we are to be dead to all things, both good and bad, in order that we should be alive to God. This is always inward; it cannot be outward. Then we are to be as though we have been raised from death back into the external world. This is no longer internal, but external: the flow is from the internal to the external.

Second, we have spoken of the indwelling of the Holy Spirit, which is in the inward man. The very word "indwell" signifies that it is internal. Then comes the fruit of the crucified, risen, glorified Lord, which flows into the external world through my body, whether it be the lips, speaking a word, or whether it be my hand with a hammer, building a shelter for someone who needs it.

Third, love is inward. We say we are to love God enough to be contented. We are to love man enough not to envy. Those are internal, but they flow out into the external world in action.

Fourth, the reverse of all this. The blows of the battle from the external world of man fall upon me outwardly. The blows fall in many ways—severe ostracism, the locking of a door, the burning of a book, a sharp word or a frown. All of them come upon me in the external world, but if they stayed in the external world of my body, as though it were a machine, they would bring no tears to me. Instead they flow through my sense, my body, into that which I am in my thought-world. And as these blows come to my thought-world, I either say "Thank you" to God, as we have already considered, or I rebel against him. In either case, the result is soon seen in the external world:

Fifth, we have spoken of active passivity, and as such we have spoken of Mary in the birth of Christ. Here is what Mary Baker Eddy says in *Science and Health* about the virgin birth: "Those interested in Christian Science have reached the glorious perception that God is the only author of man. The virgin mother conceived this idea of God and gave to her ideal the name of Jesus. That is, Joshua, or Savior. The illumination of Mary's spiritual sense put to silence material law and its order of generation, and brought forth her child by the revelation of truth." That is horrible, absolutely horrible. Mary thought of the idea, it argues, and she brought it forth. But nothing could be further from the truth. That is simply not what occurred. What occurred is that the angel came to Mary and told her that she was going to bring forth, not something showing the immateriality of the material world, but the opposite. The Holy Spirit conceived in the womb of the virgin Mary the baby Jesus Christ—including his very real body. But while Mary Baker Eddy is wrong, let us not forget the other aspect, that of active passivity. The first word that came from the angel reached Mary, and in the thought-world she made a decision. She did not say, "I want" or "I demand my own will"; she raised herself to God and gave her body to God as the handmaiden of the Lord.

"Behold the handmaid of the Lord; be it unto me according to thy word " (Luke 2:38). Mary first of all faced these things in her mind. If she had said no, there is no reason whatsoever to think that the Holy Spirit would have brought forth physically—truly physically, in her womb—the body of Jesus Christ. Now this is absolutely, totally unique: there is only one space-time virgin birth. But in another sense, as we pointed out, this active passivity is our place. In our thought-world, we are to bow under the work of the Holy Spirit internally, and then as we, in active passivity, give up ourselves to him, the fruit of the resurrected and glorified Christ flows forth through our bodies into the external world.

Now let us notice two things concerning ourselves—two things in answer to Eastern thinking, whether it has Western names or not, and to purposeless modern thinking. The first of these is that we are created within a finite limit; we cannot create as God created, yet it is wonderful beyond words that I, with all my limitations, am able to bring forth truly into the external world; that I am influencing, from my thought-world, as a true first cause, something that then stands here in stone or paint or steel or wood or in the lives of other men. However, the second thing must equally be said. That is, even after I am a Christian, I can be *a death-producing machine;* though I have life, eternal life, if I yield myself to Satan instead of to Christ, I can be an instrument of death to this external world. How sublime to be a man, made in the image of God! But how sobering, that I can bring forth out of my thought-world into the external world either that which leads to life or that which produces death in other men.

Here, then, are three conclusions:

First of all, we must understand that the reality of communion with God, and loving God, must take place in the inward self. There is no use talking about loving God except to understand that it takes place in the inward world of our thoughts. Even communication with men and women must be through the body into the area of the thought-world. If a man and a woman have only an external contact, this cannot be called communication. It is only mechanical. But a real, personal communication never remains external. It always goes back into the personality. This is true in the area of married life, the man-woman relationship as God meant it to be. Merely to have physical contact is not communication on a personal level. This must flow back into the area of personality. Only then it can be called communication. Thus real communication with man and love of man centers in our thought-world. The results may be external and the expression is external, but the love is internal. The same is true in our love for God. The result can be external, but love itself is always internal. If Christians can only learn this, very many problems concerning the Christian life would assume a different perspective. Let us understand how important is the world of thoughts. It is this that distinguishes me as a man, in contrast to machines. This is what I am, and my calling is to love God with all my heart and soul and mind.

The second conclusion is that the real battle for men is in the world of ideas, rather than in that which is outward. All heresy, for example, begins in the world of ideas. That is why, when new workers come to L'Abri, we always stress to them that we are interested in ideas rather than personalities or organizations. Ideas are to be discussed, not personalities or organizations. Ideas are the stock of the thought-world, and from the ideas burst forth all the external things: painting, music, buildings, the love and the hating of men in practice, and equally the results of loving God or rebellion against God, in the external world. Where a man will spend eternity depends on his reading or hearing the ideas, the propositional truth, the facts of the gospel in the external world, and these being carried through the medium of his body into the inner world of his thoughts, and there, inside himself, in his thought-world, either his believing God on the basis of the content of the gospel or his calling God a liar. This is not merely a mystical, existentialist experience. It is not the "final experience" of a man like Carl Jaspers put in religious terms; it is not the hallucinatory drug experience, without content. It can be expressed rationally. It is ideas; it is the content of the good news. But as far as what it means to a man is concerned, it is whether he accepts it or rejects it in the thought-world that makes the difference: if he believes God, or if he calls him a liar.

It is for this reason that the preaching of the gospel can never be primarily a matter of organization. The preaching of the gospel is ideas, flaming ideas brought to men, as God has revealed them to us in Scripture. It is not a contentless experience internally received, but it is contentful ideas internally acted upon that make the difference. So when we state our doctrines, they must be ideas and not just phrases. We cannot use doctrines as though they were mechanical pieces to a puzzle. True doctrine is an idea revealed by God in the Bible and an idea that fits properly into the external world as it is, and as God made it, and to man as he is, as God made him, and can be fed back through man's body into his thought-world and there acted upon. The battle for man is centrally in the world of thought.

The third conclusion, and the shortest of the three, is that the Christian life, true spirituality, always begins inside, in our thought-world. All that has been said in our earlier study of being free in the present life from the results of the bonds of sin is meaningless jargon, no more than a psychological pill, without the reality that God thinks and we think, and that at each step the internal is central and first. The spiritual battle, the loss of victory, is always in the thought-world.

CHAPTER 10

SUBSTANTIAL HEALING OF PSYCHOLOGICAL PROBLEMS

In the past chapter we discussed the problem of the thought-life. Now we are going on to consider the Christian life in relation to psychological problems. This is the problem of man's separation from himself, and his relationship to himself in the world of thought. Now as God is a person who thinks, acts, and feels, so I am a person who thinks, acts, and feels. But that person is a unit. I can think of my parts in various ways: as body and spirit, or as my physical part and my spiritual part. I can quite correctly think of a division of myself of intellect, will, and emotions and it is right that I should think so, because these things are open to observation. But we miss the biblical concept if we miss its emphasis that man is not just the parts, but he is a unit. Our thinking should start there. There is a Francis Schaeffer who is neither just a collection of isolated parts, nor yet just a flow of consciousness. Anything that hurts that unity is destructive of the very basic thing that man is and what man needs to be.

Once I begin to feel this, I begin to see something far, far beyond our usual restriction of the concept of sin merely to a forensic element. The forensic element is there very strongly, because God is holy, and must declare me guilty, but sin is not just a legal matter. It is something more.

The truth is not just an abstract truth; there is a truth of what I am. Now we could think of two basic areas in considering the question of man. The first is Being, or the question of his existence. This is the dilemma of all men, regardless of what their philosophy is. It is the basic thing which no man can escape, that he does exist. Endless problems are thrown up to the non-Christian man as to the question of his existence, of his Being. No matter who he is, no matter what his philosophy is, he exists and there he is. He cannot ever escape this dilemma, even by committing suicide, because if he commits suicide he may think that he can cease to be. But even in his own thought forms, suicide does not erase the fact that he has been. So we can think first of all of the problem of Being.

The second area relates to what man is in the circle of his existence. In other words, I am, but what am I in comparison with what God is? I exist, and God exists: what is the difference between the circle of my existence and the circle of his existence? And on the other side, what is the difference between my existence and the existence of the animals, plants, and unconscious materials? Because they also exist. So now we have bare existence, and then differentiations of myself from God on one side and the animals, plants, and machines on the other side.

In the area of bare existence there is no rational answer without the personal Creator, the God of the Bible. I am not saying here that there is no rational answer without the *word* "God," because one can have the word "God" without its having the content of the infinite-personal God who is the Creator as the Bible presents him. So it is not the word "God" that is the solution. It is the existence of this God of the Bible—without the existence of this personal Creator, there is no rational answer to bare existence as such. There is no answer without an infinite reference point of a personal nature. Man needs two things as he wrestles with this question. He needs an infinite reference point, but even an infinite reference point is not high enough. The infinite reference point must be of a personal nature, and that is what the God of the Bible is. On the other hand, when as a Christian I bow before this God who is there, then I can move out of the only logical position that the non-Christian can hold, and that is he must dwell consciously but silently in the cocoon of his being, without knowing anything outside of himself. This is the final dilemma of positivism of any variety. It is a hopeless situation: if he is going to be really, rationally, and intellectually consistent, he can only dwell in a silent cocoon; he may know he is there but he cannot make the first move out of it.

Now when a Christian bows before God, he can move out of this with rationality in place. The other man, man without God, if he is going to be absolutely consistent to his position, may know that he exists, but nothing else. He cannot know that anything else exists. His problem is that he cannot live so; and no man does. Man logically and rationally cannot live in this cocoon of silence. So he is immediately damned in his intellect, not just by God saying, "You are a sinner," but *by the being that he himself is*. God has made him rational. He cannot move from this cocoon and yet he must—and so he is crushed by what he is. It is not just a legal act of God that says "You are guilty"—though that is there. What man is has separated him from himself. The tension is within man. On the other hand, when a Christian bows before the personal Creator for whom man's very existence shouts aloud, then there stretches from his feet to the end of infinity a bridge of answers and reality. That is the difference.

The Christian position states two things: that God is there, this infinite-personal God; and that you have been made in his image, so you are there. There is from your feet all the way to the infinite an answer that enables you to make the first move out of your intellectual cocoon. God has spoken, and what he so teaches is a unity with what he has made. Beginning with these two things there is a bridge stretched before you, as the moon stretches a silver bridge across the ocean, from the curve of the horizon to yourself.

Now then, the wonder is that these answers do not end simply with an abstract, bare, scholastic understanding of Being, though that would be wonderful in itself. They end in communion with the infinite-personal reference point who is there, God himself. And that is tremendous. Then you can worship. This is where true worship is found: not in stained-glass windows, candles, or altar pieces, not in contentless experiences, but in communion with the God who is there—communion for eternity, and communion now, with the infinite-personal God as Abba, Father.

All of this is introduction; it is a parallel to what follows. We must now ask what I am, as a man. One could give several answers, but "rational and moral" is probably the best thing to say in the twentieth century. I am, I exist, but I exist specifically as rational and moral. Immediately I am distinguished on the left hand and on the right, as it were. First of all, I am separated from God, because he is infinite and I am finite. He exists, and I exist; he is a personal God, and I have been created personal in his image. But he is infinite, and I am finite. On the other hand, I am separated from the animals, the plants, and the machines because they are not personal, and I am personal. So if I am to begin to realize my dilemma in the present life, my separation from myself, it is good to ask, "Who am I?" I am personal, I am rational, and I am moral. On the side of my personality, I am like God; but on the other side, I am like animals and machines, because they too are finite. But I am separated from them because I am personal, and they are not.

Now the rebellion of man is trying to exist outside the circle in which God made him to exist. He is trying to be what he is not. But as he tries to be what he is not, all the elements of what he is as man rise up against him. When man stands before judgment, and God judges him, everything that man is has already risen up and judged him in the present life.

Let us think of this in two areas: on the one hand, in the area of rationality. In this area man tends, and never more so than in our own generation, to rely on a leap of absolute mysticism for the real answers, such as the problem of the unity of the whole and the purpose of man. He says on the one hand, "Why does existence have to be seen rationally? Why not just accept it as irrational?" Yet he is damned by himself. By the way God has made him, he understands that there must be some unity. So every man has the tension within himself, brought about by what God has made him as a rational man. In contrast to the animals and machines, he is rational and his very rationality damns him. Beginning by not bowing to God, with a loud shout of rationality he ends with a jump in the dark. Yet as he jumps in the dark his own rationality is always there to demand a basic answer to the unity of the detail, and thus he is constantly embarrassed, constantly torn within himself. It is not enough for him to begin with himself and work outward. This demands an infinite rationality. So the point I am making here is that in the area of rationality there is a natural separation of man from himself.

In the area of morality, we find exactly the same thing. Man cannot escape the fact of the motions of a true right and wrong in himself: not just a sociological or hedonistic morality, but true morality, true right and true wrong. And yet, beginning with himself, he cannot bring forth absolute standards and cannot even keep the poor relative ones he has set up. Thus in the area of morality, as in rationality, trying to be what he is not, as he was made to be in relationship to God, he is crushed and damned by what he is.

Think of it in another way. We can say personality is shown by that which thinks, acts, and feels. Thinking we have already dealt with under the terms of rationality, but let us think of writing. Here is will and action—but everything cuts across my will. I would do a certain thing, but I cannot put my will into infinite action, unlimited action. Even in the small area of a painter's canvas, I cannot do it. I cannot have an unlimited action in the smallest things in life, let alone the largest. And so if I am demanding infinite freedom, whether it is in the whole of life, or in a small area of life, I cannot have it; I cannot be God in action and practice. So again I fall to the earth, crushed with natural tensions in myself, and I lie there like a butterfly that someone has touched, with all the lovely things gone from the wings.

It is the same in the area of feeling, the emotions. There is no better illustration of this than the example of Freud and his fiancée. Freud, not really believing in love—saying that the end of all things is sex, but yet needing real love—writes to his fiancée: "When you come to me, little Princess, love me *irrationally.*" I have often said that no sadder word could be written, coming from such a man as Freud. Freud himself at this particular place comes to what I would call a shuddering standstill. He is damned by what he is, by the emotions of *real* love in himself, because he has been made in the image of God. So again we come to the fact that there are these separations in man from himself, as he has revolted against God.

Thus, in rebellion, not staying within the circle of what man is but trying to move into the circle of the existence of God, man falls crushed within himself at every turn. At that point he has two possibilities, and just two, if he is going to stay in the circle of rationality. He can return to his place before the personal Creator, a personal creature before a personal Creator. Or else he can go lower than his place. This second choice is not made on any necessary intellectual grounds based on facts, but because of his rebellion man chooses to go lower rather than return to his proper place as a creature before the absolute Creator. So he chooses to go lower, for he must either go back or go down. Man in revolution against the God who is there has no pointing finger, like the Renaissance paintings of John the Baptist, pointing upwards. So sinful man takes his place among the lower circles of existence; he moves down from being man into the lower existence of the animals and the machines. Man is thus divided against and from himself in every part of his nature. Think of it in any way you will—he is divided from himself in his rebellion, in rationality, in morality, in his thinking, in his acting, and in his feeling. By rebellion he is divided from God by true moral guilt, and he is damned by what he is, by wanting to be God and not being God because he is finite. He is also damned because he cannot hide among the animals and the machines, where he would try to hide. He still bears the marks of the image of God. He is damned on both sides, in both directions, simply by what God has made him. Every part of his nature speaks and calls out, "I am man." No matter how dark the night of his soul in his rebellion, there are voices that speak from every part of his nature, "I am man; I am man."

It is no wonder, then, that by the Fall man is not only divided from other men (as Cain kills Abel, for example), but is also divided from nature and *from himself.* At death the body and soul will be separated for a time, but God has also put a witness in the present life, in that the individual man in many ways is divided from his body even now. As I read the curse that God placed upon man in Genesis 3, it is quite obvious that a large section of the curse falls upon man's division from himself *now.* The emphasis here is largely physical, but it certainly carries more with it:

Unto the woman he said, I will greatly multiply thy sorrow and thy conception; in sorrow thou shalt bring forth children [she is divided from her own body] *and thy desire shall be to thy husband, and he shall rule over thee. And unto Adam he said, Because thou hast hearkened unto the voice of thy wife, and hast eaten of the tree, of which I commanded thee, saying, Thou shalt not eat of it: cursed is the ground for thy sake* [this is a curse external to himself, in nature]; *in sorrow shalt thou eat of it all the days of thy life; thorns also and thistles shall it bring forth to thee; and thou shalt eat the herb of the field; in the sweat of thy face shalt thou eat bread, till thou return unto the ground; for out of it wast thou taken: for dust thou art, and unto dust shalt thou return. (Genesis 3:15-19)*

At death there is a division from the body, but this separation does not wait till death. There is a division in man from nature and a division from himself here and now. It is not only that man is divided from his body; he is divided from himself in the thought-world of which we spoke. Man in the present life is divided in his personality. Since the Fall there is no truly healthy person in his body, and there is no completely balanced person psychologically. The result of the Fall spoils us as a unit and in all our parts.

Now into this situation comes the modern non-Christian psychologist, trying to bring an integration into the thought-world. But the non-Christian psychologist, by the very nature of what he believes, will try to bring about an integration on the level of the original rebellion. Or at the most he will try to root it in an upper-story leap, without a base. He cannot go beyond that. As a result, the integration will be an attempt to relate what is broken in the person to the animals and the machines, or it will ask for a romantic leap. Now this does not mean that there are no details that we can learn from these psychologists; there is much to learn from their insights, because they are brilliant men and good observers, but the whole does not meet the need, for it treats man as that which he is not. It is rather like having a very fine motor mechanic and, because we see certain similarities between the physical structure of man and a machine, turning over all our physical healing to him. There could be insights that the doctor might get from the motor mechanic! But the total would not be enough. The basic questions and problems remain to swing forward and upward again. Thus a man must hide from these things deep in himself, and as he does so these things make new divisions and new scars. At some level of consciousness, man cannot forget that he is man; he cannot totally deny his true rationality or his true morality.

Surely at this point there should be a cry within us. Surely there must be a real answer in this life to the separation from myself. Or is there nothing which is real? And the answer is, "Yes, thank God, there is." I think the key, in a way, is asking the question: How is it that the psychologists who act as if God is there, but merely pragmatically, like Carl Gustav Jung, are able to help their patients to some degree? I think that it is because that which really helps is always in the direction of the reality of what is. At least a man like Jung has the word "God." Or behind that, there may be at least a sense of some universal purpose, accepted blindly and irrationally, as Viktor Frankl does. And this is in the proper direction, especially in the case of those who at least use the word "God," and so it helps. To these men these things are a piece of theater; but without their knowing it, it is in the direction of what is. In fact, *he is there*, a personal God who is holy in a moral sense. Not bowing, they do not acknowledge him, and yet pragmatically they find they must act as if he is there.

Now just as in the area of the problem of being, the bowing of man in the cocoon of his consciousness opens a bridge all the way before him, so when we see what is involved here, we see we must also truly bow at this point of the divided self, and a bridge of understanding and practice opens before us.

At this point we must make an important distinction. There is indeed purely psychological guilt, in the poor things that we as men in our rebellion have become. I feel that often evangelical Christians are very harsh here. They tend to act as though there were no such thing as psychological guilt. But there is, just as there are broken bones. Psychological guilt is actual and cruel. But Christians know that there is also real guilt, moral guilt before a holy God. It is not a matter *only* of psychological guilt; that is the distinction.

When a man is broken in these areas, he is confused, because he has the feelings of real guilt within himself, and yet he is told by modern thinkers that these are only guilt "feelings." But he can never resolve these feelings, because while they *are* merely guilt feelings, he also has true moral awareness and the feeling of true guilt. You can tell him a million times that there is no true guilt,, but he still knows there is true guilt. You will never find a person who does not still find these movings somewhere in his conscience.

Earlier we have discussed the question of salvation from our consciences. We have seen there is a strong parallel between justification and salvation from the conscience. I come now as a Christian; I call the specific sin sin; I claim the finished work of Christ; I can say, "Thank you" to God, and my conscience can be at rest. Let us notice that in this process the real guilt is not overlooked, it is not swept under the rug. Real guilt is placed in a completely rational framework, and it is met within the framework, with intellect and feelings of morality meeting each other, without any fracture between them. With all rationality in place, and consciously in place (on the basis of the existence of God and the finished, substitutionary work of Jesus Christ), my real guilt now is not overlooked, but is accepted as my responsibility because of my own deliberately doing what I know to be wrong. Then it is reasonably, truly, and objectively dealt with in Christ's infinite substitutionary work. Now I can say to my conscience, "Be still!" Thus real guilt is gone and I know that anything that is left is my psychological guilt. This can be faced, not in confusion, but to be seen as part of the misery of fallen man.

To say that there is no real guilt is futile, for man as he is knows that there is real moral guilt. But when I know the real guilt is really met by Christ, so that I do not need to fear to look at the basic questions deep inside myself, then I can see that the feeling of guilt that is left is psychological guilt and only that. This does not mean to say that psychological guilt is still not cruel. But I can now be open with it—I see it for what it is—without that awful confusion of real moral guilt and psychological guilt. This also does not mean that we will be perfect in this life psychologically any more than we are physically. But thank God, now I can move; I am no longer running on ice, that is the difference. It does not need to be the old, endless circle. It is not any longer the dog chasing his tail. The light is let in. Things are orientated, and I can move as a whole man, with all the rationality I possess utterly in place. I will not expect to be perfect. I will wait for the second coming of Jesus Christ and the resurrection of the body to be perfect morally, physically, and psychologically; but there now can be a substantial overcoming of this psychological division in the present life on the basis of Christ's finished work. It will not be perfect, but it can be real and substantial.

Let us be clear about this. All men since the fall have had some psychological problems. It is utter nonsense, a romanticism that has nothing to do with biblical Christianity, to say that a Christian never has a psychological problem. All men have psychological problems. They differ in degree and they differ in kind, but since the Fall all men have more or less a problem psychologically. And dealing with this, too, is a part of the present aspect of the gospel and of the finished work of Christ on Calvary's cross.

A very practical thing for ourselves and for those whom we would help is that it is not always possible to sort out true guilt from psychological guilt. At this point the iceberg concept is a valid concept. This always was important, but today it is more important because men are thinking in this direction. We are constantly brought face-to-face with the concept of the subconscious, which is a realization that man is more than that which is on the surface. All too often the evangelical Christian acts as though there is nothing to man except that which is above the surface of the water.

Since the Fall, man is divided from himself, and so since the Fall, there is that which I am that is below the surface. We can think of it as the iceberg—one-tenth above, nine-tenths below—in psychological terms, the unconscious or the subconscious. I am not to be surprised that there is something that I am that is deeper than that which is on the surface. Here I am—the iceberg. As we said previously, it is not possible to say *at this given moment,* "I know that I am perfect—free from all known sin." Who can know perfectly what he knows about himself, as man now is? This is true even at our best moments, and it is doubly true when psychological problems and storms break over us as they surely will break over all people, including Christians. When someone comes to you in a psychological storm, and he is really torn up, it is not only unreasonable but it is also cruel to ask him, in every case, to sort out what is true guilt and what is psychological guilt.

We all have our problems, we all have our storms, but some of us can have exceedingly deep storms. In the midst of these storms that break over us, it is beautiful to know that we ourselves do not need, in every case, to sort out true guilt from psychological guilt. We are not living before a mechanical universe, and we are not living just before ourselves; we are living before the infinite-personal God. God does know the line between my true guilt and my guilt feelings. My part is to function in that which is above the surface, and to ask God to help me to be honest. My part is to cry to God for the part of the iceberg that is above the surface and confess whatever I know is true guilt there, bringing it under the infinite, finished work of Jesus Christ. It is my opinion, and the experience of many of God's children, that when one is as honest as one can be in dealing with what is above the surface, God applies this to the whole, and gradually the Holy Spirit helps one to see deeper into himself.

We may know, as the value of Christ's death is infinite, so all the true guilt in us is covered, and the guilty feelings that remain are not true guilt, but a part of these awful miseries of fallen man: out of the historic fall, out of the life of the race, and out of my own personal past. The comprehension, moment by moment, of these things is a vital step in freedom from the *results* of the bonds of sin, and in the substantial healing of the separation of man from himself.

CHAPTER 11

SUBSTANTIAL HEALING OF THE TOTAL PERSON

In the last chapter we referred to a *substantial* healing. I want to point out that when we use the word *substantial,* we must recognize two things. The first thing is that there is the *possibility* of substantial healing, but the second is that "substantial" does not mean "perfect."

The Bible makes the possibility of miracles very clear, and our experience confirms this teaching. We have seen miracles in which God reached down into history and completely healed, either physically or psychologically, at a certain point of time. But we must point out that both Scripture and experience show that while sometimes God does this, sometimes he does *not.* This is not always a matter of faith, or of the lack of faith. God is personal, and he has his own purposes. Just because a person is not healed physically, we must not assume that this necessarily implies a lack of faith.

Let us notice that even when God does heal a person perfectly in one illness, that person may not be in perfect health. Here is a person with a hernia, let us say, who is completely healed of the hernia in answer to prayer. God has done this miracle in answer to prayer, in response to faith, and according to his own purpose. But this does not mean that this person is now at all points physically perfect. He may have a headache that very night! Thus, even such a miracle falls properly under the term substantial. It is exactly the same with psychological healing. A person may be healed psychologically, but that does not mean he will be psychologically perfect the rest of his life. I often think of Lazarus after he was raised from the dead. He surely had physical sickness after this; he may have had psychological depression; and we must remember that eventually he died again. The results of the fall continue until the second coming of Christ.

If we refuse to move—physically, morally, or psychologically—short of perfection, we will not have what we can have. At this point there is danger that even the Christian may want to be God; that is, he may consciously or unconsciously set a standard of superiority, based on the unusual value he puts on himself. Sometimes we do this to ourselves, and sometimes our families do this to us. A family may place undue pressure upon a child of the family by expressing abnormally high expectations of behavior or achievement—just because the child is a child of *their* family. Often when one hears the cry, "I am not equal to others," in reality the cry means, "I want to be better than others, and I am not." Let us be careful to be honest at this point. It is dangerously easy to have within ourselves, as Christians, the old longing to be God—so that we cry within ourselves, "I should be superior because of who I am." We deny the doctrine of the Fall, and we build a new romanticism if we fail to accept the reality of our limitations, including our psychological struggles. Thus we lose the "substantially" in beating ourselves to bits trying to be what we cannot be.

I am not to set myself at the center of the universe and insist that everything bend to the standards that I have set upon my own superiority. I am not to say, "I must be thus," and if it is not thus, there is nothing but psychological despair. Some people are totally caught in this, but all of us have something of it within ourselves, swinging pendulum-like between conceit and despair.

This is true not only in the psychological area, of course; it is true in all the relationships of life. One does not have to have had much pastoral experience to have met married couples who refuse to have what they can have, because they have set for themselves a false standard of superiority. They have set up a romanticism, either on the romantic side of love or the physical side, and if their marriage does not measure up to their own standards of superiority, they smash everything to the ground. They must have the ideal love affair of the century just because they are who they are! Certainly many of the multiple marriage and divorce situations turn upon just this point. One couple refuses to have less than what they have set as a romantic possibility, forgetting that the Fall is the Fall. Another may want sexual experience beyond what one can have in the midst of the results of the Fall. You suddenly see a marriage smashed—everything gone to bits, people walking away from each other, destroying something really possible and beautiful—simply because they have set a proud standard and refuse to have the good marriage they can have.

We wait for the resurrection of the body. We wait for the perfect application of the finished work of Christ for the whole of man. We wait for this, but on this side of the Fall, and before Christ comes, we must not insist on "perfection or nothing," or we will end with the nothing. And this is as true in the area of psychological problems as it is in all other areas of life.

Having said that, let us add that we are not to go to the other extreme, and expect *less* than to act in the circle of the being God made man to be—that is, in his own image, rational and normal. What does this mean? Well, let us think of Pavlov's bell. Pavlov's bell was the beginning of the experimentation of a mechanically conditioned reflex. He rang a bell in front of the dog before he fed him, and after proper conditioning, the saliva came to the dog's mouth any time the bell was rung. This is perfectly correct concerning dogs, for that is what dogs are and what God made them to be. But woe to man when he begins to act as though this is all there is to man, because we have not been made in this circle of creation. We have been made in the circle of creation in the image of God—not only moral but rational.

The understanding of a conditioned reflex in regard to man has its limited place. If I study my physical structure, mechanics has its place in regard to the tension of the muscles and so on. But this is not all there is to man. If you deal with a man merely as a structural machine you miss the point, and if you deal with a man merely as a set of psychological conditionings, you miss the central point. Consequently, as Christians begin to deal with psychological problems, we must do so in the realization of who man is. I am made in the image of God; this being so, I am *rational* and I am *moral*, thus there will be a *conscious* and *responsible* behavior. We must not think we can simply trigger ourselves or others into mechanical reflexes and all will be well. If we begin acting this way we will deny the doctrines that we say we believe. In action that comes anywhere near the heart of psychological problems, there will be a *conscious* aspect, because God has made man this way.

The basic psychological problem is trying to be what we are not, and trying to carry what we cannot carry. Most of all, the basic problem is not being willing to be the creatures we are before the Creator. Let us imagine that you meet Atlas and he is carrying the world on his shoulder. In classical mythology he has no problem in carrying the world on his shoulder, because he is Atlas! You meet him walking somewhere on the shores of North Africa, where the Atlas mountains are. He sees you coming and says, "Here, you carry the world for a while." And you are squashed. You are squashed because you cannot carry what you have been handed. The psychological parallel is that man is trying to be the center of the universe and refuses to be the creature he is. He is trying to carry the world on his shoulder and is crushed by the simple factor that it is too much for him to bear.

There is nothing complicated about it; he is squashed in trying to bear what no one except God himself can bear because only God is infinite.

The squashing can come in various ways. When you pump too much air into a weak tire, it will blow out. The reason for this blowout is the excessive pressure, but the actual break comes at the point of the weakness in the tire. Since the Fall, we all have points of weakness. With some of us it tends to be physical; with some it tends to be psychological. If we carry what we cannot, the blowout will come and it will come at the place of our inherent weakness. The central, overwhelming pressure is that of needing to be the integration point of all things because we are not willing to be the creatures we are. We refuse to acknowledge the existence of God, or—even though acknowledging his existence intellectually—in practice we refuse to bow before him in the midst of our moment-by-moment lives.

Christian doctrine speaks first in rational answers, and then in practice, to the psychological results of man's revolt since the fall. In other words, it is not necessary to search for psychological healing outside the total structure of Christian doctrine. The Christian gospel is the answer not only theoretically but also in practice within the unity of the biblical teaching, and specifically within the unity of the creature-Creator relationship, and the redeemed-Redeemer relationship. Within the structure of the unity of biblical teaching there is the possibility not only of theoretical psychology, but also of a practical psychology.

One of these psychological results of man's rebellion is fear. Fear can come in many guises, but generally it comes in three areas: the fear of the impersonal; the fear of nonbeing; and the fear of death. We can think of other types of fear, but many fears will fit under these headings. Fear can be small, or it can be the horror of great despair. Or it can be anywhere in between these extremes. Many modern men who have come to a philosophy of despair have gone through such a horror of great darkness. Many psychologists, for example, Carl Gustav Jung, will meet this fear simply by telling the patient to act as if God were there. In his last interview, about eight days before his death, Jung defined God as "whatever cuts across my will outside of myself, or whatever wells up from the collective unconscious within myself." And his advice was, just call it "God," and give in to "him." In other words it is acting *as if.*

But in the unity of the biblical teaching, God really is there. He is not just the father-image projected, but the Christian system begins with the comprehension and declaration of his objective existence. Consequently, there need never be a fear of the impersonal. But if men do not have this God, they are eventually faced with only a stream of energy particles. Or, if they shut themselves up and put on blinders to this conclusion, they are shut up to a faceless humanity. And the more they become aware of humanity the more they realize its facelessness. Out of this springs a real fear of the impersonal, and they are right to be afraid.

But the solution for the Christian is that there need never be a fear of the impersonal, because the personal-infinite God is really there.

This is not just a piece of theater. If we live in the light of the doctrine that we say we believe, this very basic form of fear dissolves away. This is what the Christian parent says to the little child who is afraid to be left alone when the mother goes out of the room. There is nothing complex about it. It is as simple and profound as God's existence. The little child is afraid to be left alone in the dark with the impersonal situation, and we may stay there and comfort him, but eventually the Christian parent has to say, "But you do not have to be afraid, because God is here." This is a profound truth, not just for children. Indeed, it is the glory of the Christian faith that the little things are profound and the profound things are overwhelmingly simple.

So when the mother teaches the little child that God is there with him, and as the child grows and comes to know for himself that there are good and sufficient reasons to know that God is there, this has meaning in a profound sense that will prove sufficient all his life, through all his philosophic wanderings, as well as in the darkness of the night. On the basis of the existence of the biblical God, and who he is in the total structure of the Christian faith, it is not meaningless for the little child in the dark and it is not meaningless for the most diligent student in philosophy who has ever walked through the darkness of philosophical speculation. There need be no fear of the impersonal.

The second basic fear is the fear of nonbeing. Why are so many people today caught in the fear of nonbeing? Because modern man does not have any idea where he came from, and not having any answer to Being, is eventually locked up in the sequence of pure chance. Therefore he has a fear of nonbeing, and well he might. But the Christian, in the total system of Christianity, has the answer to Being, as we have already seen. Knowing the answer to Being, there is no fear of nonbeing. I have been created by an infinite-personal God, created truly outside of himself. So I know who I am in my being. I have a valid existence. That being so, there is no reason or need for a fear of nonbeing. There is a reason to fear hell if I am in revolt against God, but there is no fear of nonbeing.

The third basic fear is the fear of death. And I deal with this last because it is the most obvious fear, and because in the Christian perspective it is obvious that we should not and need not be afraid of death. To Christians there is a continuity of life on a straight horizontal line from this life on into the world to come. The chasm is past at the new birth. Death is not the chasm; we already have passed from death to life. In earlier chapters, we have stood at the Mount of Transfiguration and there we have seen the continuity in space and time. There is the Ascension; there is Stephen seeing Jesus; there is Paul seeing Jesus on the Damascus road; there is John having seen and heard Jesus on Patmos. Consequently, it should be very obvious to the Christian, inside the total unity of Christian doctrine, that there does not need to be a fear of death.

But now we are dealing with the practical problem, because this is not just a theoretical thing. And we must say that sometimes in the midst of psychological upheaval these truths are difficult to apply. But there is a rational framework within which we can work, think, and talk, and that is altogether different from the situation of a man who is in rebellion against God. What is needed in a time of psychological disturbance, whether it is temporary or more prolonged, is that we should help each other to act upon the total unified Christian teaching. This is entirely different from trying to work by jumping into the dark without a rational framework. We must talk to each other, we must help each other to think in the light of the truth of the total unified Christian system. In this we now have a point of conversation and contact in the total framework that will not give way under our feet. This is a very different thing from a psychologist sitting there smoking his pipe and urging his patient to roll his fears upon him personally on the basis of his own authority and personality, especially when you know he has his problems too.

I should like now to touch on another area of conflict and tension: the area of feelings of superiority and inferiority in relationship to other people. Many of us move backwards and forwards between superiority and inferiority, almost like the swing of a pendulum. This is a question of comparisons between myself and other men, arising from the fact that we are social creatures. No man lives to himself; no man lives on a desert island by himself. We shall be considering this in regard to communication with other men later, when we deal with the Christian's relationship to others. But at this point we are confining ourselves to the internal results of feelings of inferiority and superiority. Superiority feelings are a pushing of my status in relationship to other men, as though I were not one creature among other equal creatures. For the Christian, status and validity do not rest upon relative relationships to other men. As a Christian I do not have to find my validity in my status, or by thinking myself above other men. My validity and my status are found in being before the God who is there. My basic validity and my basic status do not depend upon what men think of me. So the problems of superiority are set in a completely different framework and I can deal with them without fearing that if I limit my superiority, my value, validity, and status will be totally lost.

It is much the same with inferiority. Inferiority is the reverse, the return of the pendulum of the clock after I have hung my superiority on the wall, as it were. If I realize the reality of my being a creature, I shall not begin with the expectation of being either unlimited and infinite, or better than others. I know who I am. I am a creature. I see myself in the light of having been created by God and in the light of the true, historic fall. So I understand that this is what I am and what all other men are. This is an entirely different starting point. I do not have to set up a desire or an expectancy that I am intrinsically superior and then feel inferior because I do not reach it. If there is anything that throws the windows open and lets the sun in, it is this. The struggles of superiority and inferiority in the total framework of the biblical teaching can be healed in just as profound a way as guilt feelings. As Christians, by the grace of God, let us act upon what we say we believe.

Christianity has another strong point here, and that is that when I find these marks of tension or conflict upon me, there is something that can be done about them. Whatever may be the mark of sin in me at any point, whenever I find these marks upon me in any situation, I am not at a dead end, because the blood of Jesus Christ can cleanse me from all true guilt, not just once, but as many times as I need. There is always the possibility of a truly new start within a totally rational framework. Thank God that there is always this possibility, upon the basis of the infinite value of the blood of Jesus Christ shed on Calvary's cross.

Finally, let us consider some aspects of a positive psychological hygiene. As a Christian, instead of putting myself, in practice, at the center of the universe, I must do something else. This is not only right, and the failure to do so is not only sin, but it is important for me personally in this life. I must think after God and I must will after God. To think after God, as he has revealed himself in his creation and especially as he has revealed himself in the Bible, is to have an integrated answer to life, both intellectually and in practice. On any other basis I do not have this. On any other basis but this I am shut up to that phrase I find in Ecclesiastes, that under the sun "all if vanity." When by the grace of God I think after God, I can have intellectual integration. I no longer need to play games of hide-and-seek with the facts that I dare not face.

Now the same is true in the integration of my personality, of the whole man. I must will after God. There is only one integration point that is enough, and that is God himself. As Paul wrote to the Ephesians, "Be not drunk with wine wherein is excess, but be filled with the Spirit, speaking among yourselves in psalms and hymns and spiritual songs, singing and making melody in your heart to the Lord" (Ephesians 5:18-19). Paul is talking here about wine as a false integration point. In contrast, if I have the Holy Spirit as my integration point and through him as the agent of the Trinity I am in communion with the whole Trinity. I can have joy and peace, and a song. I do not have to go along whistling to myself in the dark; there can be songs in the night that come from the inside out. Now this example uses wine, but we can understand here that it is not only wine, and becoming drunk. It is also any other thing that is made to be my final integration point instead of God himself. In my university days I put many a man to bed who tried to find his integration point in alcohol, and I had to give him a cold shower at four o'clock in the morning because of his thick head. "Excess"—there is no real joy in it. This is trying to find an integration point that is not enough in itself. And any other integration point besides God will lead to the same end. This is not just a theological or psychological trick. This is what I am. And nothing less will integrate the whole me, because that is what I was made for: to love God with all my heart, soul, and mind. Being in any other relationship is not enough. There are parts of me that are not encompassed by any other relationship.

There are many points of false peace and integration, and it is well to recognize them. Entertainment is one. Do we understand that even *right* entertainment can be the wrong integration point and be just as wicked and just as destructive as wrong entertainment if I put it in the place of God? There is nothing wrong with sport. Many sports are beautiful, but if sport becomes my integration point and my whole life turns upon knocking one second off my time on a downhill race, I am destroyed.

It is the same with material things. In the Christian teaching there is nothing wrong with material things as such. We do not have an aesthetic system. But it is perfectly possible for a Christian to be a materialist, with his car or his stereo set. The man who tries to find his integration point of life in his possessions is the man who is a practical materialist.

Even good music and good art must not be allowed to be the final point of integration. The artist struggles to bring all his diagonals and horizontals and verticals together in his painting so that as you are looking at it you have a feeling of peace and rest. This has a place, and it is certainly not wrong in itself. But if it is a false integration point, in the sense of being the final integration point, and if your final rest in this world depends upon looking upon a well-balanced set of verticals, horizontals, and diagonals, it is a false integration point. Music is the same. Music does give us rest. It is fine to be able to put on a recording of the music which brings you to quietness, but it is not enough as the final integration. It is not only the bad thing, but also the good thing itself which can be destructive.

It is the same with sex. Much sex today is merely an attempt to find some reality in a world that appears to have no meaning whatsoever. Often it is an attempt to "touch bottom" in a universe that is thought to have no bottom. If sex is made an absolute integration point, it is totally wrong. It is not just sinful sexual relationship that I am talking about. I mean also sexual things in their right relationship, if these become our final points of rest. They are made to be a point of rest, and as such they can be beautiful, but as our *final* point of rest they are destructive. And eating is exactly the same. Compulsive eating can also become a point of final integration.

Intellectual pursuits can offer false integration points. Intellectual pursuits can be to the glory of God. But today much intellectual pursuit is not a pursuit of truth, or a search for truth, but a game—the best game one can play, more exciting than skiing or chess. We here at L'Abri believe that Christianity does have intellectual answers, and that every man deserves an honest answer for an honest question. But this is not to be the final integration point. The integration point is God himself. It is possible even for Christians to put always more intellectual questions between them and the reality of communion with God. Even right doctrine can be the false integration point. Theology today is often a superior game, just like the game of general intellectual thinking. It is a most exciting intellectual sport. If I had to choose a game to fill up the absolute vacuum of being a non-Christian and having no absolute meaning in life, in my experience I could find no game across the whole philosophical spectrum as exciting as playing the theological game. And almost all modern liberal theology is just a game; it is pure gamesmanship. But even orthodox doctrine can become merely intellectual, a final integration point, and can actually shut us off from God rather than opening the doors to him, which it is meant to do. And religious organizations, including good and true churches, and programs, which are right in their own place, become poison when they become the final end.

False integration points may seem satisfactory, only to end in that which is insufficient, with bits and pieces of the total man left out. I picture false integration points as being like a garbage can into which we try to push a man. But it is not big enough, and so we jam him down, but his head sticks out. So we lift him out and then jam him down in a different way, but this time his legs stick out. So we lift him out and jam him down again, but now his arm sticks out. We never get the whole man in. It is simply not big enough. That is the weakness of all false integration points. Because of what God has made us to be in his own image, and for a specific purpose, there will always be bits and pieces hanging out of any falsely integrated life. Psychologically this means new divisions of personality and a new necessity of escape. And in all of these false integration points for the Christian there is a loss in heaven, because there is going to be a believer's judgment, and rewards. In all these false integration points, there will be a chastising by my loving Father in the present life, because he loves me, and he wants to bring me to himself.

But here we are talking about something else as well: we see that the loss is not only in the future, and not only in the present external world under the chastening hand of the Lord to us in his love, but also *inside* ourselves in the thought-world. It bears upon the problem not only in the future, and not only in our present relationship with God in his love, but now, in my relationship to myself.

In our day we have become very aware of psychology, and of psychological problems, as we have never been before. I have already stressed that in modern psychology there are valuable insights, as these men have struggled with the problems. They often have good bits and pieces, but this is not enough without a sufficient base. If men act upon the teaching of the Word of God, and as *proportionately* men live according to the teaching and commands of the Bible, so they have in practice a sufficient psychological base. God is good to his people. To the extent that a man lives in the light of the command of the revelation of Scripture, he has a psychological foundation. Find me the faithful pastor in the old village, and I will find you a man dealing with psychological problems on the basis of the teaching of the Word of God, even if he never heard the word psychology, or does not know what it means. It is preferable to have the proper base and framework as to who man is and what his purpose is, without the bits and pieces, than to have the bits and pieces in a total vacuum.

This does not diminish the importance of learning details from the psychologist, but with him or without him, there is no real answer to man's psychological need and crushing load apart from the Creator-creature framework, the comprehension of the Fall, and the substitutionary work of Jesus Christ in history.

If I refuse my place as the creature before the Creator and do not commit myself to him for his use, this is sin. And anything else is also misery. How can you enjoy God on any other level than what you are, and in the present situation? Anything else will bring misery, a torturing of the poor, divided personality we are since the Fall. To live moment by moment through faith on the basis of the blood of Christ, in the power of the Holy Spirit is the only really integrated way to live. This is the only way to be at rest with myself, for only in this way am I not trying to carry what I cannot. To do otherwise is to throw away my own place of rest, the substantial psychological advance I as a Christian can have in this present life.

All this is not impersonal. In it all, I am not just acting "as if" I am rolling my burden on some impersonal something; rather, I am following the invitation of the infinite-personal Creator. His own invitation is expressed in 1 Peter 5:7: "Casting all your care upon him; for he careth for you." It is not an impersonal thing. You are simply following God's own invitation when he says, "Roll your cares upon me, because I care for you." It is the very opposite of an impersonal situation. You are not rolling your care upon an impersonal mathematical formula. You are rolling your care upon the infinite-personal God. Jesus says, "Come unto me all ye that labor and are heavy laden, and I will give you rest" (Matthew 11:28). This is not only an invitation to the non-Christian to come to Christ, it is a continuing invitation to the Christian as well. He is inviting us to roll these cares not upon someone else, but upon him. Once I see this, I do not need to be afraid. We would be less than truthful, I think, if we failed to acknowledge that often we are afraid to offer ourselves for God's use, for fear of what will come. But fear falls to the ground when we see before whom we are standing. We are standing in a living relationship with a living God, who loves us, and has shown his love for us to such an extent that Jesus died on the cross. Fear falls, and we have the courage to give ourselves for his use without being afraid, when we see we are not giving ourselves in the teeth of an impersonal situation, or of a world that hates us, or an inhuman world of men. We are offering ourselves before the God who loves us, and he is not a monster, but our heavenly Father. He will not leave us in the battle as a soldier discards one piece of military equipment for another, casting it into the mud. God will never deal with us in this way. He will not use us as a weapon, without care for the weapon itself. In his hand, not only will we be useful in the battle, but even the blows brought upon us in the battle will bring us closer to himself, because he is infinite and personal, and because he loves us.

As I bow in my will in practice in this present life, it ends with communion with God as Abba, Father. Communion with God requires bowing in the area of knowledge. But communion with God also requires bowing *in my will* in these areas we have studied in these chapters. We are justified if we have accepted Christ as Savior. But present communion with God requires continual bowing in both the intellect and the will. Without bowing in the intellect, in thinking after God; without acting upon the finished work of Christ in my present life; and without bowing in the will in practice, as the waves of the present life break over me, there is no sufficient communion with God. Without these things I am not in my place as the creature in a fallen and abnormal world. These three things are absolutely necessary if there is to be real and sufficient communion with God in the present life. In the proportion that these things are so, then a person-to-person relationship to God is in place. To the extent that these things are so in practice, I am not divided from myself and against myself. The Creator, as Abba, Father, will even now dry my tears and there will be joy. This is the meaning of true spirituality in my relationship to myself.

CHAPTER 12

SUBSTANTIAL HEALING IN PERSONAL RELATIONSHIPS

As we turn now to the problem of personality, and specifically to the elements of love and communication, the key is the fact that God is a personal God. The Christian system of thought and life begins with a God who is infinite and personal, with a strong emphasis on his personality. Because of this, personality is truly valid and central in the universe and is not just a matter of chance.

Throughout the Word of God it is made very plain that God deals with us first of all on the basis of what he himself is; and secondly on the basis of what he has made us. He will not violate that which he himself is, nor will he violate that which he has made us to be. So God himself always deals with man on a basis of personal relationship. It is always a person-to-person relationship. More than this, because God is infinite he can deal with each one of us personally as though each one was the only man who existed. He can deal with us personally because he is infinite. We also find that God's dealing with men is *never mechanical*. There are *no mechanical* elements to it. His dealing with man is also *not primarily legal*, though there are proper legal aspects to it which are founded and rooted in God's own character. The God of the Bible differs from the gods that man makes. He is a God who has a character, and that character is the law of the universe, total and complete. When man sins, he breaks that law, and because that law is broken, man is guilty and God must deal with us in this proper legal relationship. Therefore, since we have been sinners, we must be justified before we can come to God. But though God does deal with us in the proper legal relationship, nevertheless centrally he does not deal with us legally, but *personally*.

Our theme in this section is true spirituality in relation to the problem of my separation from my fellowman. It is appropriate that the first "other" we must take into consideration is God, rather than another man.

Just as God always deals with man on the basis of what God is, and

131

what we are, we should and must do the same in regard to our thoughts about God and our dealings with him. Our relationship with God must never be thought of as mechanical. That is why a strong sacerdotal system must always be wrong. We can *never* deal with God in a mechanical sense, and we should not deal with him on a *merely* legal basis, though there are these proper legal relationships. Our relationship with God after we have become a Christian must always be centrally a person-to-person relationship.

Of course, there is this distinction that must not be forgotten, that he is a Creator and we are creatures; therefore, in all my thoughts and acts toward God I must keep the creature-Creator relationship in mind. This, however, does not alter the person-to-person nature of our relationship. So the command is to love God with all our heart, soul, and mind. He is satisfied with nothing less than my loving him. I am not called merely to be justified. Man was created to be in personal fellowship with God and to love him. Prayer is always to be seen as a person-to-person communication, not merely a devotional exercise. Indeed, when prayer becomes only a devotional exercise, it is no longer biblical prayer.

Now, turning from our person-to-person relationship with God, let us think of the relationship between ourselves, that is, within our own kind. Just as it is centrally important to remember when I am dealing with God that my relationship must be kept on a creature-to-Creator basis, so when I am dealing with my own kind, I must remember that the relationship must be exactly the opposite: equal-to-equal. But though it is equal-to-equal, and not creature-to-Creator, or greater-to-less, still it should be personal. The Bible presents to us no mechanical human relationships; it allows none, because God did not make us as machines. Further, our relationship to other men must not be primarily legal, although there will be proper legal relationships between man. Though this sounds simple, it is not simple at all. Very often the sin of the church has been to forget this very point.

Now who are my kind, when I speak about those with whom I should deal on a person-to-person level? My kind are all those who have come from Adam. In Acts 17:26 we are told, "And he has made of one all nations of men, for to dwell on all the face of the earth." We who believe the Bible insist on a literal Adam, and if we do, this carries with it something that is most practical: *All who come from Adam are my kind.* This is as wide as the human race, and I am to have a person-to-person relationship, as equals, with each of those with whom I come into contact.

The Bible is explicit that mankind is divided into two classes, and only two: those who have accepted Christ as Savior, and who are therefore Christians, and those who have not accepted him: those who are brothers in Christ, and those who are not. But this must not obscure to the true Christian's thinking that his primary dealing on a personal level is to be to all men, and not just to fellow Christians. The church has always recognized this in insisting that marriage is given by God not just to the redeemed, but to all men. This is an ordinance of God to all men. Unredeemed man's sin and separation from God does not remove him from the human ordinances of God. As an example, when the Lord Jesus Christ was giving us our basic commandment concerning our fellowmen, he used the word "neighbor." He said, "Thou shalt love thy neighbor as thyself." At this point there is to be no distinction between Christian and non-Christian. I am to love my neighbor, every man, as myself. And he made very plain what he meant by this in telling the story of the Good Samaritan (Luke 10:27-37). It is most significant that the last of the Ten Commandments uses the same word; it says we are not to covet anything of our neighbor (Exodus 20:17). Every man is my neighbor and is to be treated in a proper human, man-to-man relationship. Every time we act in a machinelike way towards another man we deny the central teaching of the Word of God— that there is a personal God who has created man in his own image.

Or we can put it in another way. I have said that the last screen in our thinking and in our life must be nothing other than God himself. The last screen, the last point of our thinking, must not be just things *about* God, it must be a relationship with God himself. The same must be true in our thinking of men. The last screen cannot be anything less than the individual and personal relationship, in love and communication. The command is to love him, not just to think about him, or do things for him. We are not to stop with a proper legal relationship—for example, to think of a man as legally lost, which he is, in the sight of a holy God—without thinking of him as a person. Saying this, we can suddenly see that much evangelism is not only sub-Christian, but subhuman—legalistic and impersonal.

Of course, we must continue to stress the other side, especially in this modern century that has no time for legal relationships. In a period of anti-law, like that in which we are living today, we must always stress that proper legal relationships are important. They are important in the area of sex and marriage; they are important in thinking of the proper legal relationship in the church, and its purity. Nevertheless, we must never lose sight of the *heart* of these relationships: recognizing the individual as a human being.

Or we can look at it in another way. Man, having put himself rather than God at the center of the universe, constantly tends to turn inward instead of outward. He has made himself the last integration point of the universe. This is the essence of his rebellion against God. Now with God this does not make a problem, for when God turns to himself, he is Trinity, and the members of the Trinity have been having love and communication among themselves before the creation of the world. So when God turns to himself as the center of the universe, there is still communication and love. But when I turn inward, there is no one to communicate with. And so each man in himself is exactly like the bullheaded minotaurus, shut up in his personal solitude in his labyrinth at Crete. This is the tragedy of man. He is not adequate and there is no one there to answer.

This not only leads to psychological problems, but it also destroys my relationship with others. On the other hand, when I begin really to think and act as a creature, then I can turn outward, as an equal, to other men. Suddenly I am no longer mumbling to myself. Once I accept myself as an equal to all men, I can talk as an equal to other men. I no longer have to talk to myself centrally and finally. If I acknowledge that I am really not God, and that since the fall we all are sinful, then I can have true human relationships without battering myself to pieces because they are not sufficient in themselves, or because they are not perfect. The trouble with human relationships is that man without God does not realize that all men are sinful, and so he hangs too much on his personal relationships, and they crush and break. No love affair between a man and a woman has ever been great enough to hang everything on. It will crumble away under your feet. And as the edges begin to break away the relationship is destroyed. But when I am a creature in the presence of God, and I see that the last relationship is with an infinite God, and these human relationships are among equals, I can take from a human relationship what God meant it to provide, without putting the whole structure under an intolerable burden. More than this, when I acknowledge that none of us are perfect in this life, I can enjoy that which is beautiful in a relationship, without expecting it to be perfect.

But most of all, I must recognize that no human relationships are going to be finally sufficient. The finally sufficient relationship must be with God himself. As Christians we have this relationship, and so our human relationships can be valid without being the finally sufficient thing. As sinners, acknowledging that we are not perfect in this life, we do not need to cast away every human relationship, including the relationship of marriage, or the relationships of Christians inside the church, just because they prove not to be perfect. On the basis of the finished work of Christ it is possible, once I have seen this, to begin to understand that my relationships can be substantially healed in the present life. When two Christians find that their relationship has hit a wall, they can come hand-in-hand and bring their failures under the blood of Christ, and get up again and go on. Think what this means practically in the areas of human relationships, in marriage, in the church, the parent-child relationships, the employer-employee relationship.

Or we can put it in yet another way. The Christian is to be a demonstration of the existence of God. But if we as individual Christians, and as the church, act on less than a personal relationship to other men, where is the demonstration that God the Creator is personal? If there is no demonstration in our attitude toward other men that we really take seriously the person-to-person relationship, we might as well keep quiet. There *must* be a demonstration; that is our calling: to show that there is a reality in personal relationship, and not just words about it. If the individual Christian, and if the church of Christ, is not allowing the Lord Jesus Christ to bring forth his fruit into the world, as a demonstration in the area of personal relationships, we cannot expect the world to believe. Lovelessness is a sea that knows no shore, for it is what God is not. And eventually not only will the other man drown, but I will drown, and worst of all, the demonstration of God drowns as well when there is nothing to be seen but a sea of lovelessness and impersonality. As Christians, we are not to be in fellowship with false doctrine. But in the very midst of the battle against false teaching, we must not forget the proper personal relationships.

Every time I see something right in another man, it tends to minimize me, and it makes it easier for me to have a proper creature-creature relationship. But each time I see something wrong in others, it is dangerous, for it can exalt self, and when this happens, my open fellowship with God falls to the ground. So when I am right, I can be wrong. In the midst of being right, if self is exalted, my fellowship with God can be destroyed. It is not wrong to be right, but it is wrong to have the wrong attitude in being right, and to forget that my relationship with my fellowmen must always be personal. If I really love a man as I love myself, I will long to see him be what he could be on the basis of Christ's work, for that is what I want or what I should want for myself on the basis of Christ's work. And if it is otherwise, not only is my communication with the man broken, but my communication with God as well. For this is sin, breaking Christ's second commandment to love my neighbor as myself.

This remains true even if the man is desperately wrong and I am right. When 1 Corinthians 13 says, "Love rejoices not in iniquity," it means exactly what it says. When we find another man to be wrong, we are not to rejoice in his iniquity. And how careful I must be, every time I see a situation where I am right and another man is wrong, not to use it as an excuse to scramble into a superior position over that man, rather than remembering the proper relationship of fellow creatures before God.

The next practical question must be, if I am to see myself as an equal to all other men, and I live in a fallen world in which there has to be order imposed, where is this order to come from? Men have wrestled with this through the centuries. But I would suggest that from a scriptural viewpoint this is not really a difficult question, though it is a most practical one. The Bible makes a distinction between man as a creature and the relationship God has set up as offices among men. The central thing is the command in the Ten Commandments, "Honor thy father and thy mother." This is the core of the whole matter. There is a proper legal relationship between the parent and the child. But that does not mean that when the proper legal relationship is in order, everything is perfect. Far from it. Although my child is honoring me, the parent-child relationship may not have come to full fruition. The children are to love the parents, and the parents are to love the children on a personal level, within the legal framework, and once we see this, we understand all that follows. This is a relationship of office, but between *fellow human beings.* If we could learn this, we would stop seeing the tragedy of poor parent-child relationships. My child, while he is still a minor, is my fellow creature created on my own level; I am not intrinsically higher than he is. For a certain number of years there is to be this other relationship of office, but I am never to forget, as I look at my child, even when I hold that child in my own arms, that that child is a creature, created on my own level. And more than this, if he becomes a Christian while he is my minor child, I must not forget that then he is not only my fellow creature, but he is also my brother or my sister in Christ.

And the child is not just to have the proper legal attitude toward the parents; he is to work for a personal relationship to them, in love. Anything less than the personal relationship between the parent and child is not only wrong; it is full of sorrow.

Here is the New Testament teaching on human relationships:

And be not drunk with wine, wherein is excess; but be filled with the Spirit; speaking to yourselves in psalms and hymns and spiritual songs, singing and making melody in your heart to the Lord; giving thanks always for all things unto God and the Father in the name of our Lord Jesus Christ; submitting yourselves one to another in the fear of God. Wives, submit yourselves unto your own husbands, as unto the Lord. . . . Husbands, love your wives, even as Christ also loved the church, and gave himself for it. . . . So ought men to love their wives as their own bodies. He that loveth his wife loveth himself. For no man ever yet hated his own flesh; but nourisheth and cherisheth it, even as the Lord the church. . . . For this cause shall a man leave his father and mother, and shall be joined unto his wife, and they two shall be one flesh. . . . Let every one of you in particular so love his wife even as himself; and the wife see that she reverence her husband. Children, obey your parents in the Lord: for this is right. Honour thy father and mother, which is the first commandment with promise; that it may be well with thee, and thou mayest live long on the earth. And, ye fathers, provoke not your children to wrath: but bring them up in the nurture and admonition of the Lord. Servants, be obedient to them that are your masters according to the flesh, with fear and trembling, in singleness of your heart, as unto Christ; not with eyeservice, as menpleasers; but as the servants of Christ, doing the will of God from the heart; with good will doing service, as to the Lord, and not to men: knowing that whatsoever good thing any man doeth, the same shall he receive of the Lord, whether he be bond or free. And, ye masters, do the same things unto them, forbearing threatening: knowing that your Master also is in heaven; neither is there respect of persons with him. (Ephesians 5:18-22, 25, 28, 29, 31, 33; 6:1-9)

In each case mentioned here there are two parts: the legal framework, and a strong personal relationship within that legal framework. This is true of the marriage relationship, of parent and child, and of employee and employer. It is interesting to notice that the Bible also gives us a legal relationship in regard to those who govern us in the State. But even in this there is a personal relationship involved in our praying for these people.

The church is not to be a place of chaos; it is to be a place of order. We read in 1 Peter 5:1-3: "The elders which are among you I exhort, who am also an elder, and a witness of the sufferings of Christ, and also a partaker of the glory that shall be revealed: feed the flock of God which is among you, taking the oversight thereof, not by constraint, but willingly; not for filthy lucre, but of a ready mind; neither as being lords over God's heritage, but being examples to the flock." Here we see in the relationships of the church of the Lord Jesus Christ that there is relationship of office, but in the midst of this Peter pleads with the elders to keep the personal relationship alive and real. Thus there is to be an order in the church, just as there is to be an order in the family and an order in the State. There needs to be an order of office, but in every single office that is presented in the Scriptures there is the personal emphasis within that legal concept. In the church the elder is an office-bearer. But both the preaching elders and the ruling elders are "ministers," and the word "minister" is a personal relationship, it does not speak of dominance. There is to be order in the church, but the preaching elder or the ruling elder is to be a minister, with a loving personal relationship with those who are before him, even when they are wrong and need admonition.

In the area of office, whether it is in the church, in the home, or in the State, the relationship indeed must be personal. Man is a rebel and there needs to be order in this poor world, but when I use whatever office God gives me, whether it is in the state, the church, or the home, or as an employer, it is to be for God's glory and for the other person's good. If I must make legal judgments in my position as having an "office" in one of the relationships of life, I must consciously show that all I can do is let the Bible speak. I have no intrinsic authority in myself; I am an equal creature with the other person, and I too am a sinner. And every time I come into a place of eminence of office, I am to do it with trembling, because I must understand from the Word of God that eventually I will give account of my stewardship, not only in regard to my proper legal relationships but on the basis of my personal relationships.

One of the problems with humanists is that they tend to "love" humanity as a whole—Man with a capital M, Man as an idea—but forget about man as an individual, as a person. Christianity is to be exactly the opposite. Christianity is not to love in abstraction, but to love the individual who stands before me in a person-to-person relationship. He must never be faceless to me or I am denying everything I say I believe. This concept will always involve some cost. It is not a cheap thing, because we live in a fallen world, and we ourselves are fallen.

Now we must ask, what happens when someone has been hurt by my sin? The Bible teaches that the moment we have confessed this sin to God, the shed blood of the Lord Jesus Christ is enough to cleanse the moral guilt. As Christians we insist that all sin is ultimately against God. When I hurt the man, I sin against God. But let us never forget that this does not change the fact that because man has been made in the image of God, the man I have hurt has real value. And this must be important to me, not only as a concept but in my practice and demonstration. My fellowman is not unimportant: he is God's image-bearer. That is true of the non-Christian man as well as of the Christian. He is lost, but he is still a man. Thus when God says, "My child, this sin is different; in this sin you have hurt another person," I respond, "What shall I do, Lord?" And the answer is clear from the Word of God: "Make it right with the man you have hurt. The man you have hurt is not a zero."

But what is the usual reaction when God says to me, "Go and make it right"? It is to answer, "But that would be humiliating." Yet surely, if I have been willing to tell God I am sorry when I have sinned, I must be willing to tell this to the man I have hurt. How can I say, "I am sorry" to God, if I am not willing to say, "I am sorry" to the man I have hurt, when he is my equal, my fellow creature, my kind? Such a repentance is meaningless hypocrisy. This is why so many of us have deadness in our lives. We cannot just trample human relationships and expect our relationship to God to be lovely, beautiful, and open. This is not only a matter of what is legally right, but of a true relationship of person to person on the basis of who I am and who the man is.

In James 5:16 we are told, "Confess your faults one to another." We are not told to confess our faults to a priest, not to the group, unless the group has been harmed, but to the person we have harmed. This is a very simple admonition, but in our present imperfect state, very difficult to obey. To go and say, "I am sorry" is to enter by the low door: first in confessing to God, and then to the individual harmed. Let me emphasize, this is a *person* before me, a human being, made in God's image. So it is not such a low door after all, because all it involves is being willing to admit our equality with the one we have hurt. Being his equal it is perfectly right that I should want to say, "I am sorry." Only a desire to be superior makes me afraid to confess and apologize.

If I am living in a real relationship with the Trinity, my human relationships become more important in one way, because I see the real value of man, but less important in another way because I do not need to be God in these relationships any longer. So now I can go up to a man and say, "I am sorry for such and such specific harm I have done you," without smashing the integration point of my universe, because it is no longer myself, but God. And we do not need to wait for the big explosions, especially among brothers and sisters in Christ. We do not need to wait for someone else to begin. This is being what we should be, and it should be moment by moment.

This is communication. The men of the modern world are asking whether personality is real, whether communication is real, whether it has meaning. We Christians can talk till we are blue in the face, but it will all be meaningless unless we *exhibit* communication. When as a Christian I stand before a man and say "I am sorry," this is not only legally right and pleasing to God, but it is true communication on a highly personal level. In this setting, the human race is human.

Of course, confession to God must always come first. It is confession to God and bringing sin under the shed blood of Christ that cleanses us—not confession to man. We must always stress that, over and over again, because men get confused. But this does not change the fact that after there has been confession to God, *then* there must be real communication in a man-to-man, personal relationship with the person I have hurt.

We must be careful of three things in this connection. First, we must be careful not to do it merely to be seen of men or the church, because then the whole thing becomes worse than it was in the first place; it is a mere show.

Second, we must see that sometimes this will mean going back for years. If we have lost the human relationship, in the church, the family, or in general, almost always it means that years ago we have got off the track in some personal relationship. In talking about the freedom of our conscience in reference to sin before God, we said that we have to go back to where we sinned, to where we got off the track, even if it was twenty years ago. The same thing is true in human relationships. If I know that somewhere back in my life I have dealt with some Christian, or some non-Christian, on less than a really human basis, I must go back if possible, pick up the pieces, and say, "I am sorry." Many can vouch for the fact that there have been springs of living water and dews of refreshment when they have gone back, knocked on somebody's door, and apologized—even after many years.

I do not think there are many people with any sensitivity who cannot remember some doors that need knocking on, and some apologies that need to be made.

Third, we must remember that Christ's crucifixion was real and in the external world. In Philippians we are told: "Let this mind be in you, which was also in Christ Jesus" (2:5). Christ's crucifixion was on a hill, by a road, where everybody who passed by could not only see his pain, but also his shame. It was not done in a shadow, hidden away somewhere. And when you and I have some concept of really living under the blood of the Lord Jesus Christ, our confession to God and to man must be as open as Christ's crucifixion was open on that hill, before the eyes of man. We have to be willing for the shame, as well as the pain, in an open place. It is not enough merely to agree with the principle as we deal with these personal relationships; we must put it into practice. Only in this way can we give a demonstration to a watching world, in a way that they can understand, that we live in a personal universe, and that personal relationships are valid and important. Only thus can we show that we are bought by the Lord Jesus Christ not just in theory, but in practice, and that there can be substantial healing of the separation between men in the present life, and not just when we get on the other side of death. And if the other man is not a Christian that makes no difference. The demonstration and the reality is to be on our part, not his.

In two areas above all others the Christian demonstration of love and communication stands clear: in the areas of the Christian couple and their children; and in the personal relationships of Christians in the church. If there is no demonstration in these two places, on the personal level, the world can conclude that orthodox Christian doctrine is nothing but dead, cold words. In a psychologically oriented age people may try to explain away individual results in a Christian life, but love and communication between Christians add a human dimension which, especially in a day like ours, is not easily explained away.

When man sinned, certain legal strictures were placed by God upon man and woman in marriage. In order to give a framework for order in the midst of a fallen world, the woman and man stand face to face with each other as creatures, yet the man has an office in the home. But the man-woman relationship must not only be stated in the negative—either in regard to wrong order in the home or concerning committing adultery, as important as these negatives indeed are—but it must also contain the command and the reason to love. Marriage is a picture of Christ and his church (Ephesians 5:23). How poor is our concept of the work of Christ if we make it only a legal thing. How poor not to understand that we are to have communion with Christ and that there is to be a mutual love between him, the bridegroom, and ourselves, the bride. If human marriage is meant to be a picture of that tremendous union of Christ and his church and of the present relationship of Christ as bridegroom to the church as bride, surely then there should be a showing forth of joy and a song in communication and love between man and woman.

We are finite, and therefore do not expect to find final sufficiency in any human relationship, including marriage. The final sufficiency is to be found only in a relationship to God. But on the basis of the finished work of Christ, through the agency of the Holy Spirit and the instrument of faith, there can be a real and substantial healing of relationships, and thus true joy.

As Christians we understand something more. Not only are we finite, as we were created, but since the fall we are all sinners; therefore we know that relationships will not be perfect. But on the basis of the finished work of Christ, human relationships can be substantially healed, and can be joyous. Christianity is the only answer to the problem of man. Modern multiple divorce is rooted in the fact that many are seeking in human relationships what human relationships can never give. Why do they have multiple divorce, instead of merely promiscuous affairs? Because they are seeking more than merely the sexual relationship. But they can never find it, because what they are seeking does not exist in a purely finite relationship. It is like trying to quench thirst by swallowing sand.

If man tries to find *everything* in a man-woman or a friend-to-friend relationship, he destroys the very thing he wants and destroys the ones he loves. He sucks them dry, he eats them up, and they as well as the relationship are destroyed. But as Christians we do not have to do that. Our sufficiency of relationship is in that which God made it to be, in the infinite-personal God, on the basis of the work of Christ in communication and love.

The same thing is true for Christian parents and their own children. If we try to find everything in human relationships or if we forget that neither we nor they are perfect, we destroy them. The simple fact is that the bridge is not strong enough. To try to run on to the bridge of human relationships that which it cannot bear is to destroy both the relationship and ourselves. But for the Christian, who does not need to have everything in human relationships, human relationships can be beautiful.

Love is the interplay of the whole personality. The relationship is personal, and the whole personality of man is the unit of the soul and the body.

The Bible teaches that there is such a thing as a continuation of the spirit, after the body dies. but we must be careful not to be platonic here. The emphasis in the Scripture is upon the unity of the man, the unity of soul and the body. And with communication—substantial, though not perfect—the body is the instrument. Actually there is no other way to have communication, except through the body. But in marriage this becomes a very special thing to understand. Sexual love and romantic love are both equally out of place if they are extramarital and therefore outside of the proper legal circle. Both are wrong, and equally wrong. And if either is the "all" even with the proper legal relationship, they must dwindle and end in an agony or a search for variety; but if the couple stand as personalities—personality facing personality—within that which is the proper legal circle, then both the romantic and the sexual has its fulfillment in the full circle of what we are, in thinking, acting, and feeling.

In such a setting, the Song of Solomon is a part of the song of triumph, "The Lord has triumphed gloriously." The enemy, the devil, has been dumped into the depths of the sea. Human marriage between Christians is supposed to be this. There is a ring of life within the legal circle of marriage. There is to be joy and beauty in the interplay of the total personalities.

Sin has brought a division between man and woman, and thus their bodies tend to be separated from their personalities. To the extent that we live thus, we are less than man was meant to be. If we as Christians live with this separation, we are saying that the twentieth-century man is right when he says, "We are only animals or machines." In the animal world the sexual relationship at its proper moment is enough, but it is never so with man. The *personal* is needed. The thing must be seen as a whole, as a unity, within the legal circle, but with the reality of communication and love.

If love and communication are not present in marriage, how can there be the next step, the person-to-person relationship between parent and child? This should grow from the substantially restored relationship of the husband and wife. This parent-child relationship too has its legal aspects. But again, it is not primarily legal, it is personal. With husband and wife, and then parent and child, the personal is meant to be central. The legal bonds are first in each case, because we do have a God who has a character and who is holy. But within the legal bonds, communication is to be there and love is to be there. With the addition of a child in the home, love and communication are no longer only reciprocal, but take on profound diversity.

Where the wife and husband are Christians, they are also brothers and sisters in Christ, as well as lovers—"My sister, my spouse!" (Song of Solomon 4:4, 9, 12). And then the children are added, also as brothers and sisters in Christ, as they grow a bit older and accept Christ's death for themselves. In such a setting what Christian would want to marry an unbeliever?

The call is not to all Christians to be married, but the call is to all Christians to show forth to a watching world the reality of the interplay of personality. There is a relationship of man to man, woman to woman, friend to friend as Christians and in the church of Christ that can also show forth the substantially restored human relationship. There was a oneness of the early church, that, while it was not perfect, nevertheless was a present reality. And as we read of their oneness in the Scripture and hear the words that were spoken concerning them, "Behold, how they love one another," we see that this was a practical oneness, not just a theoretical unity.

How beautiful Christianity is—first, because of the sparkling quality of its intellectual answers, but second, because of the beautiful quality of its human and personal answers. And these are to be rich and beautiful. A crabbed Christianity is less than orthodox Christianity. But these human and personal answers do not come mechanically after we are Christians. They come only on the level of what God made us to be in the first place, and that is personal. There is no other way to have these beautiful answers. They cannot be achieved mechanically, or by only standing in a proper legal circle, as important as that is. They grow In the light of what we say we believe as orthodox Christians: that we are creatures, and that while we are not perfect in this life, even after becoming Christians, yet through moment-by-moment faith in the finished work of Christ on the cross, beautiful human relationships can and do come forth. There must be orthodox doctrine, true. But there must also be orthodox *practice* of those doctrines, including orthodoxy in the human relationships.

I hesitate to add, but I will, that this is *fun*. God means Christianity to be fun. There is to be a reality of love and communication in the Christian-to-Christian relationship, individually and corporately, which is completely and truly personal.

CHAPTER 13

SUBSTANTIAL HEALING IN THE CHURCH

Let us now examine true spirituality in relation to our separation from our fellowman, particularly in the church of the Lord Jesus Christ.

There is a strong tendency in current theology to speak of the resurrection of Jesus Christ in terms that totally equate it with the beginning of a church, referred to as "his Body." This is pernicious and confusing. The Bible insists that this is not the case, and that Jesus was raised physically from the dead. However, let us never forget that according to the teaching of the Word of God, the church is spoken of as the body of Jesus Christ. We must not forget the one, in rejecting the other. "For as we have many members in one body, and all the members have not the same office: so we, being many, are one body in Christ and every one members one of another" (Romans 12:4-5). We are one body, in Christ. "For as the body is one, and hath many members, and all the members of that one body, being many, are one body, so also is Christ. For by one Spirit are we all baptized into one body, whether we be Jews or Gentiles, whether we be bond or free; and have been all made to drink into one Spirit. For the body is not one member, but many" (1 Corinthians 12:12-14).

So Jesus Christ rose physically from the dead, and also the church was born at Pentecost in the particular form in which we now know it. It is, in very specific ways, his body. And as his body, the church should exhibit him to the world, until he returns. Just as our bodies are our means of communication to the external world, so the church as the body of Christ should be Christ's means of communication to the external world. We think our thoughts and then we convey our thoughts to the external world through our bodies; our physical body is the point of communication with the external world and this is the way we affect the world. So the church, as the body of Jesus Christ, is called to be the means whereby he may be exhibited and whereby he acts in this external world until he comes again. Since the fall of man there have been two humanities, and not just one. There are those who are still in revolution against God, and there are those who by God's grace have returned to him on the basis of Christ's work. The church should be the reality and the exhibition of this distinction, in each generation. There should never be a moment when any generation can say, "We see nothing of the exhibition of a substantially restored relationship between men in this present life." Every single generation should be able to look to the church of that generation and see an exhibition of a supernaturally restored relationship, not just between the individual and God, though that is first; not just between the individual and himself, though that is crucial; but between man and man, in the church.

"Church" in Greek (*ekklesia*) simply means "that which is called out," called out of a lost humanity. That is the calling of the church of Jesus Christ. In our generation in the arts, in music, in philosophy, in drama, everywhere you turn, man is coming to see that man is less than he knows he should be. Our generation sees this, but the problem is not new in our time. Ever since the Fall, rebellious man has been this way. And the church is called out of this humanity, in order to be humanity before a lost humanity.

The basic thing is not organizational unity, though it has its place. The human body is directed by the head. The hands are not in direct relationship with each other. The reason they cooperate is that each of the hands, each of the joints, each of the fingers, is under the control of a single control point, and that is the head. Block the body from the head and the body is spastic; the fingers, for example, could never find each other, and uniformity of action would come to an end.

It is exactly the same with the church of Jesus Christ. The real unity is not basically an organizational unity; the real unity is not of one part with the other parts, but a unity in which each part is under the control of the Head and therefore functions together. The unity of the church is basically the unity of the Head controlling each of the parts. If I as an individual, or if groups of Christians, are not under the leadership of the Head, the church of Jesus Christ will be functioning like hands that cannot find each other; the whole thing will be broken and a "spastic" situation will exist in which the church functions in a most disjointed way. This is true not only in the whole church of the Lord Jesus Christ, but it is also true in any specific group of Christians. A specific local church, a specific school that is supposedly Christian, a specific mission, or whatever you are talking about—proportionately as each of the Christians of that group fails to be under the leadership of the Holy Spirit, under the headship of Christ, that group will proportionately be spastic.

Remember the two chairs. As I am living individually in the supernatural, moment by moment there will be individual results, and an individual exhibition. But equally, as we are living as a corporate body in the light of the supernatural, there will be corporate results and an exhibition. It is not only that the individual should so think and live, but the whole group as a group should be attuned to living consciously, moment by moment, in the reality of the supernatural. Then there is the exhibition; then there is the result there should be.

There is a very special calling, a special oneness in Christians working together—a unity that is not merely organizational or abstract. It will not be perfect in this life, because the Bible does not say we are going to be perfect in this life, but on the basis of the finished work of Christ there should be a substantially restored relationship among Christians in this life. Thinking of these things, we come to some immediate practical considerations. First of all, as the church exhibits who and what God is to each generation, there must therefore be a proper legal emphasis. God does have a character. We are not exhibiting a God who is "the unknown God," in the sense taught by Tillich. God has a character. And because he has a character, there is to be an exhibition of that character, and this means functioning in the proper legal circle. The proper legal aspects of the church will deal first with doctrine, because otherwise the body is telling lies about its Head.

The next step is that in the proper legal circle there will be a dealing with the life of both the individual and the group. The legal aspects are not arbitrary. They are rooted in God's existence and in his character, concerning which he has spoken to us in the Bible. The church is not a body that thinks up ideas; the church is a declarative statement of what God has revealed concerning himself in the Scripture. So the legal aspects are fixed by God himself. The church should represent the supernaturally restored human race in reality, and as such it is very obvious that there must be the proper legal circle of those in the church in distinction to those not in it.

Many stress that a Christian must not marry a non-Christian, but then they are willing to be in a church where many, including the outstanding officers, openly reject the God of the Bible. To try to have proper love and communication that would please God in such a condition is like trying to have a sexual life that would please God with another man's wife or woman's husband. The proper legal circle must be first or the church in name is not the church in reality. Men will not always be led to apply the same action at the same moment in regard to the Bible's command concerning the practice of the principle of the purity of the visible church, but if the principle is given up as such, the proper legal circle falls to the ground just as certainly as if we cast aside Christ's and the Bible's command concerning the proper legal aspect of marriage.[1] So the church has its legal relationships in regard both to doctrine and life.

But though the legal is important and has its proper place, it is not all. Within the proper legal relationship of the church, the person of God and his full character are to be set forth by words and exhibition. Only God is infinite and finite man cannot exhibit that. But as we are made in his image, individually and together we are called upon to exhibit the fact that he is personal. This we can do; it is our calling. Because of the Fall it will not be perfect exhibition—we must keep saying that. But as Christians it can and should be a true one, and of all relationships this is most certainly the calling of the church as the body of Christ.

The matter of the proper legal circle, the battle against false doctrine and sin, will never come to an end in this life. But the proper legal relationship, while right in itself, should be only the vestibule to the reality of a living, personal relationship, first the group with God and then between those who are in the church. Really to glorify God, to enjoy him, and to exhibit him, can *never* be mechanical and can never be *only* legal, but also *personal.* When the church of Christ functions on less than the personal level, it is exhibiting less than what God is, and therefore it is less than the church should be. There should be an exhibition of redeemed human personal relationships.

The church has always put emphasis, in words, upon these things. We speak of *the brotherhood of believers,* and we have already mentioned the fact that we come into a new relationship with other Christians when we accept Christ as Savior. At the new birth, I come into a new relationship with each of the three persons of the Trinity, and I become a brother to all other Christians, to all the others who are in Christ, the family of God. It is meant to be a true brotherhood and therefore a visible demonstration of brotherhood. As orthodox Christians we reject the present emphasis that destroys the distinction between saved men and lost men. The liberal theological deliberately breaks down the difference between saved and lost. But woe to any church of Christ that is strenuous in keeping this distinction clear, but then

[1] See *The Church before the Watching World,* InterVarsity Press, 1971.

shows no sign of brotherhood. In the Apostolic Creed we state, "I believe in the communion of saints." We state this as firmly as we do the other items of the Creed. This is not to be merely a theological phrase, yet how little communion we see—how little reality. It is not just to be comprehended that it exists, and that it reaches across all space and time with all believers. There is a mystical union of saints, true enough, but the communion of saints is to be exhibited as well.

What should the church *consciously* be then? The church consciously (and my emphasis is very strongly on the word *consciously*) should be that which encourages its members in the true Christian life, in true spirituality—in that which we have set forth in this book. It should encourage them in freedom in the present life from the bonds of sin, and in freedom in the present life from *the results* of the bonds of sin. It should encourage substantial healing in their separation from themselves and a substantial healing in their separation from their fellowman, especially fellow Christians.

No matter how legally right a church is, if it does not provide an environment conducive to these things, it is not what it should be. First, the church should teach the truth, and second, the church should teach a *practice* of the existence of God, and a *practice* of the reality of and the exhibition of God's character of holiness and love. The church cannot merely teach these things in words; we must see the practice of these things in the church as a corporate body. Can faith be taught? People often ask me that, and I always have an answer: Yes, faith can be taught, but only by exhibition. You cannot teach faith only as an abstraction. There must be an exhibition of faith, if faith is to be learned. Each group must operate on the basis of God's individual calling for them—financially and in other matters—but there is an absolute rule, and that is that if our example does not teach faith, it is destructive. There can be many callings but there cannot be a calling to destroy the teaching of faith. The church or other Christian group that does not function as a unit in faith can never be a school of faith. There is only one way to be a school of faith and that is consciously to function by faith.

The church or other Christian group must also teach in word the present meaning of the work of Christ. Then as a corporate body it must consciously live on this basis. It must not think that just because the church or group is legally right, its corporate Christian life will come automatically. It never will; God does not deal with us automatically. Any Christian group must function moment by moment by conscious choice on the basis of the work of Christ, through the power of the Holy Spirit, by faith. It is not that the group just calls its individuals to so live, but that the group as a group so lives. It is death to think that things are going to come automatically just because of past legal decisions, even though they were right. There must be the present choice, a moment-by-moment choice, a conscious choice of operating on the basis of the work of Christ.

Every Christian group must also teach in words the duty to exhibit that God exists and that he is personal, and then as a corporate body practice this truth. There is a cost in this, for the church's methods must be chosen with much prayer and care, and "results" alone will not now be the sole, simple criterion. It must practice the choice of means in its work which will exhibit that God exists.

In words and practice the church must also, as a *corporate body,* show that it takes holiness and love, and love and communication, seriously. And how can it do this unless it consciously practices holiness and love, and love and communication, both toward those inside the church group and those Christians outside their group?

In short, if the church or other Christian group *as a corporate body* does not consciously seek freedom from the bonds of sin, and freedom from the results of the bonds of sin, on the basis of the finished work of Christ in the power of the Spirit by faith, how can it teach these things with integrity in words, and how can it teach these things at all by exhibition? And if the church, group, mission, or whatever it is, does not care enough to function in this way as a corporate body in its internal relations, as brothers and sisters in Christ; and then in its external human relationships to those outside the group, how can we expect individual Christians to take these things seriously in their personal lives—in the husband-wife, parent-child, employer-employee, and other relationships?

Thus the church's or Christian group's methods are as important as its message. It is to deal consciously with the reality of the supernatural. Anything that exhibits unfaith is a mistake, or may even be corporate sin. The liberal theologians get rid of the supernatural in their teaching, but the unfaith of the evangelical can in practice get rid of the supernatural. May I put it like this? If I woke up tomorrow morning and found that all that the Bible teaches concerning prayer and the Holy Spirit were removed (not as a liberal would remove it, by misinterpretation, but *really* removed) what difference would it make *in practice* from the way we are functioning today? The simple tragic fact is that in much of the church of the Lord Jesus

Christ—the evangelical church—there would be *no difference whatsoever.* We function as though the supernatural were not there.

If the church does not show forth the supernatural in our generation, what will? The Lord's work done in the Lord's way does not relate only to the message, it relates also to the method. There must be something the world cannot explain away by the world's methods, or by applied psychology. And I am not at all speaking here of external, special manifestations of the Holy Spirit, I am thinking of the normal and universal promise to the church concerning the work of the Spirit.

Here are three things which are universal promises to the church regarding the Holy Spirit. First: "But ye shall receive power, after that the Holy Spirit is come upon you: and [then] you shall be witnesses unto me both in Jerusalem, and in all Judaea, and in Samaria, and unto the uttermost part of the earth" (Acts 1:8). The word *then* is not there in the Greek, but surely the thrust of it is there. The church is not supposed to be a witness in its own power, but the universal promise to the church is that with the coming of the Holy Spirit there will be power.

Second, there is a universal promise of the fruit of the Spirit: "But the fruit of the Spirit is love, joy, peace, longsuffering [patience], gentleness [kindness], goodness, faith, meekness [gentleness], temperance [self-control]: against such there is no law. And they that are Christ's have crucified the flesh with the affections and lusts. If we live in the Spirit, let us also walk in the Spirit" (Galatians 5:22-23). If we have accepted Christ as Savior, we live in the Spirit, but let us walk in the Spirit. And these fruits of the Spirit are not some special thing; they are a universal promise, given to the church.

And the third thing that is universally promised concerning the Holy Spirit is that the raised and glorified Christ will be with the church through the agency of the Holy Spirit: "And I will pray the Father, and he shall give you another Comforter, that he may abide with you for ever; even the Spirit of truth; whom the world cannot receive, because it seeth him not, neither knoweth him: but ye know him; for he dwelleth with you, and shall be in you. I will not leave you comfortless [orphans]: I will come to you" (John 14:16-18).

Notice the words "I will not leave you comfortless [or orphans]: I will come to you." The promise of Christ—crucified, risen, ascended, glorified—is that he will be with his church, between the Ascension and his second coming, through the agency of the indwelling Holy Spirit. These are universal promises, made to the church for our entire era.

These are the things that the world should see when they look upon the church—something that they cannot possibly explain away. The church should be committed to the practical reality of these things, not merely assenting to them. There is a distinction between men, even converted men, building Christ's church, and Christ building his church through converted and consecrated men.

Organizational and financial matters should not be allowed to get in the way of the personal and group leading of the Holy Spirit. There is no use talking of these things abstractly, without bringing them down to the real place where the battles are fought. Organizational and financial arrangements of the church should not rule out the exhibition of the reality of the existence of God. Throughout church history, one is aware that the danger always comes at a time of emergency. An emergency arises which causes us to cut off the exhibition of faith, and discount the possibility of God guiding through financial matters. There always seems to be a legitimate reason for reaching out and steadying the ark. As Uzzah reached out to steady the ark, he thought he had a good reason for disobeying the word of God (2 Samuel 16:6-7). At this point, he no longer trusted God to steady the ark. Might it not fall? Might not something of God's work and the glory of God be shaken? This danger often comes in organizational and financial emergencies, when it would seem for a moment that the glory of God is jeopardized.

There is to be a moment-by-moment supernatural reality, for the group as well as for the individual. This is the really important thing. In comparison to this, everything else is secondary. We tend to think of Christ building his invisible church, and our building the visible church. We tend to think in this kind of a dichotomy. So our building of the visible church becomes much like any natural business function, using natural means and natural motives. How many times do we find that in doing the business of the Lord Jesus Christ, there is a rapid opening prayer, a rapid closing prayer after half the people have left, but in between there is no difference between doing the Lord's business and the business of some well-organized business enterprise?

Instead of that, we should always look to him, and always wait and pray for his leading, moment by moment. This is a different world. We will not do it very well—we will always be poor in this fallen world, until Jesus comes back. But the church of the Lord Jesus Christ should be functioning moment by moment on a supernatural plane. This is the church living by faith, and not in unfaith. This is the church living practically under Christ's leadership, rather than thinking of Christ being far off and building the invisible church, while we build that which is at hand with our own wisdom and power. This places the church in the supernatural battle, extending into the heavenlies, and not just in a natural battle. This raises the battle from being merely the battling of other organizations, other men, to a real battle of the church in the total war, including the unseen war in the unseen portion of reality. This makes the church the church, and short of this, the church is less than the church. With the objective standard of the Word of God, and the indwelling of the Holy Spirit, in these areas we are to be yielded to Christ.

Prayer now becomes something more than merely an abstract religious, devotional act. It is a place where the church is the church, and where Christ is in the midst in a special, definite, and real way. Organization is not wrong; let us say this with force. Organization is clearly commanded in the Word of God, and it is needed in a fallen world. But it becomes wrong if it stands in the way of the conscious relationship of the church to Christ. Simplicity of organization is therefore to be preferred, though at the same time it is all too easy to get one's eyes fixed on simplicity of organization and forget the reason for simplicity, which is that Christ may truly be the Head of the church.

In a fallen world there is need of organization, and there is also need of Christian leadership. But the leaders, as office-bearers, stand in relationship to the church of Jesus Christ, to the people of God, as brothers and sisters in Christ, as well as leaders. The church as a whole, and the officers, are to function consciously on the basis of each one being equal as created in the image of God, and as equal in the sense of being equally sinners, redeemed by the blood of the Lamb. In this way, believing in the priesthood of all true believers, believing in this supernaturally restored relationship among those who are brothers in Christ, believing in the indwelling of the Holy Spirit in each individual Christian—organization and Christian leadership do not stand in antithesis to true spirituality.

With such a mentality in the church we can also say something about the attitude of loyalty. Loyalty in the church of Christ should be in an increasing scale. To reverse the scale is to destroy the church. The primary loyalty must be to God as God, on a personal level. This is personal loyalty to the person of the living God, and it is essential and first, above all other loyalties. So strongly do I feel this that I would put the second loyalty in a decreasing scale; loyalty to the principles of revealed Christianity. It is not that I would separate these principles of revealed Christianity from the personal God, but rather that it is because they are from him that they have any authority.

Third in importance is loyalty to organizations, not because they have been called church organizations and have had historical continuity for a certain number of years, centuries, or millennia, but only as far as they are biblically faithful. Below this, in fourth place, must be that which is often put first, and that is loyalty to human leadership. It must be kept in its proper order. To reverse the order is to be totally destructive. If loyalty to human leadership becomes central, we tend to show loyalty not even to our own organization (which would be horribly limited in itself) but to our own little party *within* the organization. But if, on the other hand, we keep our eyes on loyalty to the personal God as our "first love," we will tend to love, on a practical level, all those who are Christ's.

Once more let us stress that the end to be attained in working for the purity of the visible church is loving relationship, first to God and then to our brothers. We must not forget that the final end is not what we are against, but what we are for.

Let's bring all this down to our own level. Loving the whole church is not just loving the whole church facelessly, like the humanist man loving Man but caring little about the individual. As finite we cannot know the whole church that is on the earth now, let alone the whole church across all space and time. So what does it mean to "love the church of Jesus Christ" in practice? It is very clearly laid out in the New Testament that the Christians should meet in local congregations and groups. In these churches and groups the universal church is cut down, as it were, to our own size. We can know each other on a person-to-person level and have person-to-person love and communication.

God commands that we should assemble ourselves together until Jesus comes (Hebrews 10:25). We are commanded not only to meet together, but to help each other (verse 24). Christianity is an individual thing, but it is not *only* an individual thing. There is to be true community, offering true spiritual and material help to each other. In the New Testament church the love and community extended to their responsibility under the leadership of the Holy Spirit to all the needs of life, including the material ones. In the local church, the Christians of that particular congregation are called upon to be in close contact personally. This is what stands under proper scrutiny—not only of men, but of God and the angels and demons in the unseen world. Many a Christian's child has been lost because they have seen nothing of real love and communication in that body where it may be scrutinized, in the church "brought down to our size."

This is important for modern man, who has lost his humanity. Modern man's problem is not getting to the stars; it is this loss of humanity. So here is something for modern man to look at: the interplay of true human beings in a group small enough for it to be practically possible. Of course there is an element of danger in drawing our own family out of their sterilized little social circle. There is a danger that our own little stratified rightness of thought-forms and social circle will be challenged. But what else is the community of the saints to mean? It is not just a group of strangers sitting under a roof nor a set way of provincial thinking, but whatever has real value being shaken down until eventually the real values become the values of the group and those in it. It is in this way that the upper-middle class aspect of the church in all of our countries, which churchmen everywhere are disturbed about, can be really changed: with the doors thrown open to the intellectuals, the working men, and the new pagans. There is a danger to our set ways, but within the structure of Scripture and under the leadership of the Holy Spirit there is a possibility of glory, too.

The local church or Christian group should be right, but it should also be beautiful. The local group should be the example of the supernatural, of the substantially healed relationship in this present life between men and men.

The early churches showed this on a local level. For example in Acts 2:42-46 we have something that sets the tone: "And they continued stedfastly in the apostles' doctrine and fellowship, and in the breaking of bread, and in prayers. And fear came upon every soul: and many wonders and signs were done by the apostles. And all that believed were together, and had all things common; and sold their possessions and goods, and parted them to all men, as every man had need. And they, continuing daily with one accord in the temple, and breaking bread from house to house, did eat their meat with gladness and singleness of heart."

The appointing of the deacons in the early church exhibited this, too. These men were waiting on tables, in a local situation, not just as an idea or a principle, but serving individual people at a point in space and time (Acts 6:1-5). The problem was that Greek-speaking Christian widows were being neglected in the area of material help because of a language problem; it was a real situation. It was not just an idea but real men waiting on real tables. How many orthodox local churches are dead at this point, with so little sign of love and communication: orthodoxy, but dead and ugly! If there is no reality on the local level, we deny what we say we believe, right up to the apex, because what we really deny is that God is a personal God. There must be the mentality, in the local situation, of an interest in people as people, and not just as church members, attenders, or givers. These are people, and this is related to our statement that we believe in a personal universe because it all begins with a personal God.

In the local church the possibility of the diversity of love and communication, rather than merely a reciprocal situation (as in a husband-wife relationship), expands wonderfully. In the Old Testament *the whole of life and culture* was based upon the relationship of the people of God first to God and then to each other. It was not just a religious life, but the whole culture. It was a total cultural relationship, and though the New Testament no longer sees the people of God as a state, nevertheless there is still an emphasis upon the fact that the whole culture and way of life is involved in this vital diversity of love and communication. There is to be no platonic dichotomy between the "spiritual" and other things of life. Indeed, we read in Acts 4:31-32: "And when they had prayed, the place was shaken where they were assembled together; and they were all filled with the Holy Spirit, and they spake the word of God with boldness. And the multitude of them that believed were of one heart and of one soul: neither said any of them that ought of the things which he possessed was his own; but they had all things common."

The Bible makes plain here that this is not a communism of law or external pressure. In fact, Peter, speaking to Ananias about his property, stressed: "Whiles it remained, was it not thine own? and after it was sold, was it not in thine own power?" (Acts 5:4). This sharing is not law, but true love and true communication of the whole man to whole man, across the whole spectrum of what humanity is. The same thing happened further abroad. Gentile Christians gave money to Paul to carry to Christian Jews. Why? So that there would be a sharing of material possessions. This is ten thousand times removed from the dead, cold giving of most Christians. This is not a cold, impersonal act as a bare duty, but a sharing of the whole man with the whole man. True Christian giving is in love and communication across the whole framework of the interplay between whole men.

You will remember that we have previously seen that true spirituality has meaning in all the practical relationships of life: husband-wife, parent-child, employer-employee. These things must be taught in the church as an aspect of the conscious side of sanctification, to be understood and then acted upon by choice. The environment of the local church or other Christian group must be conducive for these things to grow. Such growth will never be once for all, but, like all things in our life, a moment-by-moment process. There must be moment-by-moment teaching, there must be moment-by-moment example, of the present meaning of the work of Christ, and a conscious choice of the individual and the group to lay hold of these things. There must be faith, moment by moment, in God's promises, to lay hold of these things—first in instruction, and then in example.

The church needs to function consciously on the basis of the finished work of Christ and not on the proud basis of any inherent value in itself or any supposed or assumed inherent superiority. It must be consciously working on the basis of the supernaturally restored relationship and the exhibition of that restored relationship, and not upon merely natural gifts and talents. And if these things are forgotten or minimized on the basis of past, present, or legal relationships, the whole group can grieve the Holy Spirit just as surely as can the individual Christian. The Holy Spirit is the one by whom the body of Christ is joined together and if the body does not care about being fitly joined together, it is he who is grieved.

As in marriage, all this is possible because God himself is the ultimate reference point, and so the members of the local church do not need to hang too much on each other. The church should be what it can be, for it does not need to be what it cannot be. The pastor does not need to hang everything on the people, and the people do not need to hang everything on the pastor. Everything is to hang only one place—on him who is infinite and personal, and who can carry everything perfectly. This is not a matter of just hanging everything on doctrines *about* the infinite and the personal God, but upon him *as a person*—because he is there, and he knows the local group by name, and the individuals in the group by name.

The alternatives are not between being perfect or being nothing. Just as people smash marriages because they are looking for what is romantically and sexually perfect and in this poor world do not find it, so human beings often smash what could have been possible in a true church or true Christian group. It is not just the "they" involved who are not yet perfect, but the "I" is not yet perfect either. In the absence of present perfection, Christians are to help each other on to increasingly substantial healing on the basis of the finished work of Christ.

This is our calling. This is part of our richness in Christ: the reality of true spirituality, the Christian life, in relation to my separation from my fellowmen—including those fellow men who are my brothers and sisters in Christ—in the church as a whole and in the local congregation or other Christian group. It is not to be practiced in a dull, ugly way; there is to be a thing of beauty, observed by those within, and those outside. This is an important part in preaching the gospel to the humanity still in revolution against God; but more than this, it is the only thing that is right on the basis of the existence of the personal God and on the basis of what Christ did for us in history, on the cross.

And having come this far, true spirituality—the Christian life—flows on into the total culture.